GET THE PARTNER YOU DESERVE

How love succeeds

HERMANN MEYER

HERMANN MEYER researches partner relationships and destiny. He lives happily with his wife, the partner he deserves, for over twenty years in Germany and Austria and spends most of his free time in the USA. Following his studies of psychology and natural healing, he specialized in research on psychosomatics. He was a longtime member of the Executive Board of IPSE (Center for Research on Psychosomatics). Today he directs the Institute for Destiny Coaching in Munich, provides individual and group counseling, offers training sessions, and regularly conducts weekend seminars in several locations in Germany, Austria, and Switzerland on the topic of partner relationships and the development of personality.

Acknowledgments:

I would particularly like to thank my wife, Maria and my son, David. Without them, it would not have been possible to complete this book. They remained steadfastly at my side, offered advice, and provided crucial suggestions as well as impulses. My family has given me constructive criticisms, where revisions and distinctions have been required.

Furthermore, I would like to thank my clients and seminar participants, who, through their honesty and authenticity, have contributed to my understanding of the subconscious mechanisms in relationships

Writing this book has been an adventure of a special kind.

Table of Contents

The 7 Stages of identification

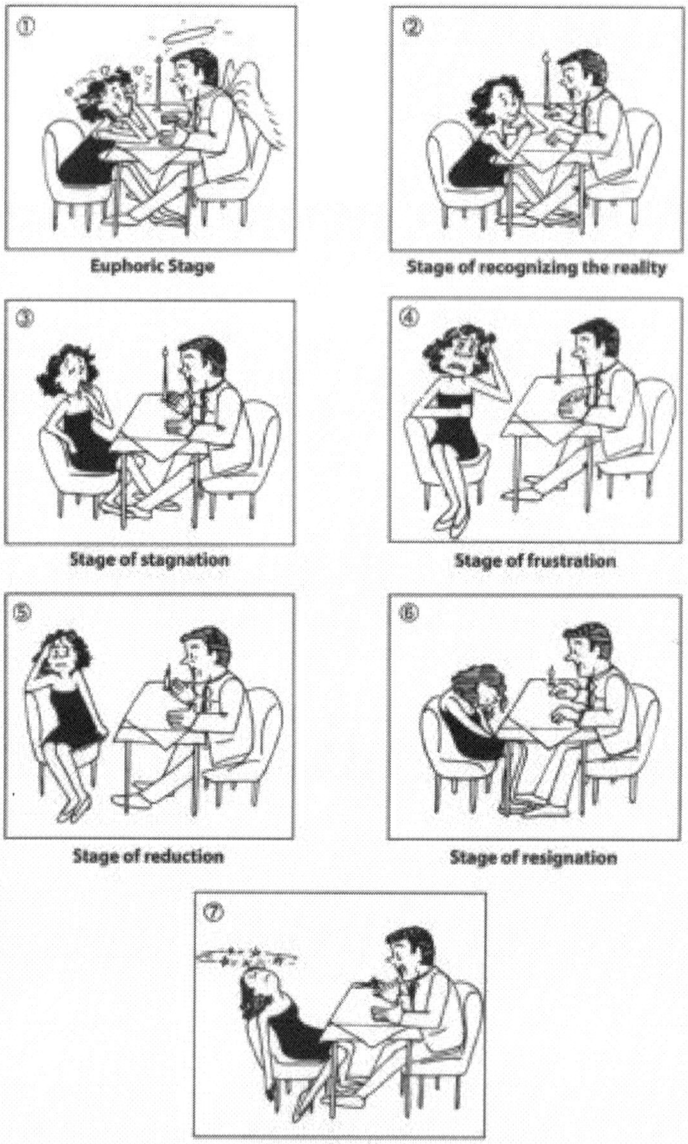

Foreword: The science of the partner relationship

Is there anyone who would not want a relationship filled with loving tenderness, thrilling eroticism, passionate sex, material and emotional security, and intellectual adventures? And yet very few of us manage to develop such a relationship. What explains this?

Most of us are convinced that a beautiful and fulfilling relationship is a gift bestowed by Fortuna, the goddess of luck.

In this book, I would like to show that the opposite is true: anyone can have – and deserve – a successful relationship.

This is because each of us is the architect of our own fortune. This is also – and especially – true when it comes to finding happiness in love. To accomplish this, we need to become aware of what must be done to achieve happiness. Even if it all appears basically quite simple, the reality is that few of us pay attention to the ground rules and basic principles of a relationship. We know that just the presence of frequent and tender hugs, snuggling at night, and loving words can have a great effect on a relationship, creating a sense of security, acceptance, appreciation. It often takes just one of the two partners to start it off, to make an investment. And yet most of the time, each waits for the other to make the first move.

Such a situation is not very different from what we understand as relationship building. Many individuals say they want to develop a relationship, though few are aware of the elements and skills required to do this. In this book, I highlight the hidden mechanisms and rules that are crucial to a successful partner relationship. To do this, it is necessary to penetrate the vast field of the unconscious, which influences 95% of our life, including our partner relationships. An examination of the unconscious mind and all that relates to it brings into focus a unique science: the science of the relationship. Of course, this science cannot claim to be scientific in the sense of the natural sciences. This is not possible, since the unconscious cannot be evaluated according to the criteria of the natural sciences – it cannot be counted, measured, or weighed. And yet the unconscious also follows rules and procedures that can assist us in learning a great deal about the inner workings of successful and broken relationships.

There is so much here that is of general interest, so much to be discovered about a man and woman and their life together that is of incalculable value to their mental and spiritual evolution. And this knowledge can spare them a great deal of suffering as individuals.

Relationship science is not a science unto itself; rather, it incorporates knowledge from a range of other sciences: biology, medicine, ecology, psychology, sociology, and others.

This book aims to contribute to the science of the relationship, given the importance of breaking through the prevailing ignorance and naïveté and shining a little more light into this darkness!

Doing so means finding answers to the following questions: Where do repressed elements need to be brought into awareness to achieve a better starting point for the relationship? Where does imbalance exist in the relationship? Where are the scales tipped because one partner invests more than the other in the relationship? Where is a mistaken belief detrimental to relationship health? When does it become necessary to abandon a projection? Where do old norms and ideals need to be challenged? Where does an inhibition or fear need to be overcome? Where should another approach be taken, or another perspective integrated? What talent or skill should be cultivated to achieve greater joy in the relationship?

Have difficulties emerged because one partner is too focused on the mainstream and not on the other's uniqueness? When does it become necessary to show understanding for the partner's individuality and for the characteristics of the opposite sex?

What is the right moment for being assertive, for respecting boundaries, for stepping back?

When is it necessary to consider seeking professional help? When is coaching sufficient and when is psychotherapy indicated?

These and other questions are posed far too infrequently in a relationship. Were they to be raised, they would lead to the realization that partners in a relationship are in no way constrained to follow the ordinary course of events; instead, each of them has much to contribute to the success of the relationship. Indeed, there is an abundance of opportunity to set a relationship on a true course through strategic and tactical maneuvering.

Hermann Meyer

Munich, May 7, 2015

PART ONE
Interpretations

The proportion of the unconscious in our actions is immense
and the rational proportion very small.
GUSTAVE LE BON

The four types of the unconscious

The animal unconscious

Sigmund Freud maintained that the unconscious influences 95 percent of our feelings, thoughts, actions, and behaviors. The unconscious can be divided into four types. The 'animal unconscious', which arose based on the denial and suppression of humans' original animal nature, has a significant influence on our lives. In general, it is fundamentally impossible for us to suppress our animal nature for long. This means that there is always a gap between the cultural human being who is alienated from his or her own nature and the human being as mammal, which the cultural human seeks to hide from others and from him- or herself. We play the role of the active, established, intelligent, informed, mobile, cool, unassuming, enterprising, careful, industrious, hard-working, harmonious, peace-loving, approachable, gentle, responsible, independent, and anxiety-free citizen, often without the slightest awareness of what powerful forces and energies are simmering beneath the surface.

The collective unconscious

According to Carl Jung, the personal unconscious rests on a deeper layer of consciousness that, in contrast to the individual psyche, contains habits and behaviors that are essentially the same. The collective unconscious comprises all the basic structures of human conceptual and behavioral patterns as a reflection of general human experience. The collective unconscious thus serves as a reservoir of possibilities for new creations and discoveries.

The personal unconscious

The personal unconscious is shaped by our parents, the environment, culture, and the times in which we live. This is the 'kitchen', so to speak, where a person's destiny is prepared. It contains all our shortcomings, traumas, repressed feelings, conflicts, emotional repertoires, reaction patterns, and beliefs. Those individuals whose feelings, thoughts, and actions are primarily influenced by these unconscious strivings are no longer subject to outside influence. Any such attempt activates their defense system and encounters resistance.

The personal unconscious exercises an incredible power – it determines the selection of one's neighborhood and even residence, one's choice of career, company or work sector, friends, and acquaintances, and of course it also plays a crucial role in selecting a partner.

As an old saying puts it, "Everything comes to us as it is decided." But it is not decided by an extraterrestrial power or transcendent being but by our own unconscious. This force is very creative in staging illnesses, daily occurrences, and all types of situations. It controls us, and it is scarcely possible for us to be creative and inventive in structuring our own lives. Or, put another way: as children, we look for love, attention, and recognition. We do everything to be able to survive within the family unit. To achieve this, the unconscious trains us in a variety of strategies and tactics. But many of these approaches, including the way we want to achieve them (such as striving for power, emotional blackmail, etc.) are usually not very pleasant and can sometimes even be destructive. An adverse situation develops if the (survival) strategies employed as a child are continued into adulthood. The individual still lives in the past and has not yet arrived in the present.

This produces what is known as compulsive repetition, a feature of the personal unconscious. It causes psychological sufferings, traumas, mindsets, beliefs, and reaction patterns to be constantly replayed. This is also the reason some people apparently have no success in relationships. It can happen that an individual only ever seeks out partners who cause the sort of psychological pain that was inflicted by a father or mother. Compulsive repetition is likewise present when an individual consistently chooses dominant, jealous, unloving, or irresponsible partners.

In that regard, Eric Berne, the founder of Transactional Analysis, developed the concept of the 'script': "A script is a continuous life plan that forms in early childhood under the strong influence of one's parents. This script constitutes that psychological force that drives human beings toward their destiny – whether one fights it or affirms it, it is one's own free will." We also derive the analogy of the player piano from Berne: "Each person sits at the player piano, moving his fingers across the keys. The piano roll, its perforations having been punched out in the time of his forebears, slowly unrolls as he plays. The music produces a sound over which we ourselves have no influence – sometimes melancholy, sometimes happy, sometimes shrill and out of tune, then melodious again. He lives under the illusion that the music is his own, and his own body, as it gradually tires from the hours and days of piano playing, gives witness to this. During the intermissions, he sometimes rises to receive the applause or boos of his friends and relatives, who likewise believe that he is producing his own sounds."

Thus, someone under the influence of an unconscious life plan or script is inalterably living life according to a program. This determines individual behavior in all key areas: career, love, marriage, parenting. In theatrical terms, family life generally forms the stage and, related to that, the backdrop and the atmosphere in the design of the life plan. As children, we experience some family members as role models, others as typical representatives of 'good' or 'evil'. The sets are created from the rooms of the house where the child grows up, or from the child's immediate surroundings.

There is a unique paradox inherent in this whole. This is because, although the personal unconscious is nothing to trifle with and is linked to an almost frightening control, it should in fact not be viewed seriously. In a person's own life, this means not taking it personally

- to be subjected to intrigues
- to be cast out
- not to be accepted

- to feel neglect
- to be unappreciated
- to be treated in an unfriendly manner
- to be devalued
- not to be confided in by a partner
- if the partner has an affair
- to be left by the partner

In all these cases, my 'ego' is still operating on the imprints from early childhood. It constantly reacts to the other person's script, which likewise stems from childhood influences and has nothing to do with the here and now. In this way, I find myself merely in my movie or play, which in no way refers to me personally. Even if, for example, I had been unwanted as a child, I am not forced to reproduce these feelings over and over – my unconscious is not required to keep on creating new scenes just for me to feel unwanted yet again.

After all, now I am grown up, and I know that I am wanted if I contribute my skills! And if, despite this, I keep falling into admittedly painful situations because the personal unconscious has still not been sufficiently refuted, I know I can make all this easier on myself if I keep in mind that such difficulties can be avoided by making them conscious.

Granted, it is important in this regard to examine whether I have developed certain resources and abilities only to become unwanted again. Or whether I am engaging in inappropriate behavior only so that I can continue to be unwelcome in the presence of others.

Frequently, the strategy of developing our mechanisms as a defense is particularly strong in those areas that expose our sore spots. It is possible, therefore, that I will refuse to grow as a way of ensuring that I will continue to be unwanted by others, since in this way I can repeatedly experience my old feelings and hurts.

One point must be clarified: do I interpret a situation in a specific way so that I can once again experience the same feelings as before? Or is it truly the case that I am unwanted? Even if the latter is true and I am in fact unwanted, I can realize that this condition of being unwanted is not reality, since I have only created this situation unconsciously, perhaps because I do not want to give up my inappropriate behavior. Because it is also true that my inner being, my true nature, is always wanted.

To recognize that the scenes of one's own life only resemble a play and that reality will be found in an entirely different place is a great relief. The key to this lies in my inner development. I must transform myself initially from an unconscious into a conscious actor and ultimately into the viewer of this play, who returns to reality once the performance has ended.

The individual unconscious

The individual unconscious is that part of our unconscious that allows access to our true self, to our true nature, and thus to the voice of life, to eternal truths.

Here too is the home of what we call common sense, the logos, and true reason. These qualities are not subject to manipulation by a political ideology or the mainstream. Those with imagination can tap into this individual unconscious in the same way they access the collective unconscious, drawing on it to form ideas for new projects and creations.

Here it is possible to be creative on our own, no longer allowing the personal unconscious – which, as we have seen in the example of the player piano, often moves in strange ways – to take our place in the creative process.

In a way, the individual unconscious offers a synthesis of the experiences of the collective (the collective unconscious) and one's own experiences (the personal unconscious). The individual unconscious is where I differentiate myself from the collective and grow beyond it. The possibility exists here for me to develop something of **my own**, and this can be done in all areas of life – intellectual distinctiveness, a sense of taste, my own opinion, my individual philosophy of life, my own structuring of leisure time ...

The development of something of one's own – beyond tradition, mainstream thinking, and current fashion – equates to consummation of what is called the **individuation process**.

To a certain extent, those who were once only a mouthpiece of those who came before, parroting their standards, morals, and conventions, can now stand up, both for themselves and for that which distinguishes them from others. The individual unconscious also contains **psychological self-healing powers**. So long as something remains unconscious, psychological self-healing powers do their work inconspicuously and quietly in the background. In the same manner as physical self-healing powers, they attempt to bring the individual back into balance.

Here it becomes evident that many of the negative occurrences that affect our lives are in fact strategies by the unconscious to achieve sought-after harmony once again.

Such incidents are generally viewed not as a rebalancing effort or healing process, nor as either a reference to something else or an appeal to get to the important part and subdue it, but rather as a more-or-less dire affliction that one simply must accept. Thus, while we believe that this occurrence in our life is throwing us off stride, it is in fact an attempt to reestablish our equilibrium.

Simply put, this means that a fear of destiny is a fear of the attempt by the unconscious to balance our one-sidedness (fixation on a single pole in a bipolar world) and our shortcomings and deficiencies. The rebalancing effort involves, therefore, moving the self-healing powers of the psyche over to our conscious and no longer allowing it to function independently and automatically but instead thwarting destiny and, in advance, consciously incorporating the opposite pole.

Thus, the individual unconscious presents a great opportunity to move ahead toward **reality**: to discover who we are and how we function, who our partner is and how he or she ticks, and what other human beings are truly like. This constitutes a singular opportunity to avoid the pull of misfortune by becoming aware of unconscious themes (what reality is like, what the inner voice of our nature and logos are saying, what the rules of life are). **Avoidance** is the first step toward reality. And over time – in other words, while developing awareness – it works increasingly well to reduce our own adamancy and arrive at free will.

I previously had no choice. Back then, whether I wanted to or not, I had to play the role that was demanded of me. Only now do I see that there are other ways of feeling, thinking, and behaving. I can make different decisions and live in a manner other than that prescribed by the old program.

Connected to this awareness is the realization that the choice of a partner is no longer predestined but can be a free choice, made by selecting from various options.

The more we bring the individual unconscious into our awareness and strengthen its influence, the weaker will be the influence of the deterministic powers and influences that originate in the personal unconscious.

Johann Wolfgang von Goethe expresses it this way:

> I happily confirm my belief that we carry within us a spark of that eternal light that must shine in the essence of our being and which our poor senses can only remotely perceive. I see it as our highest duty to bring this spark to flame within us and to achieve the divine within us.

Knowledge about the individual unconscious has a clearly important potential for restructuring a partner relationship. There are two reasons why this is so: first, it becomes easier to see the reality and to develop a different attitude regarding one's partner; and second, it will become evident that generalized relationship patterns always have adverse effects on both partners. It follows that the likelihood of building a specific sustainable relationship increases where each partner has the freedom to develop something of his or her own in different areas of life but where a common denominator can then emerge from these actions. For example, while each partner can maintain a separate lifestyle, both partners together will have their own common lifestyle specific to them. In this way, 1 + 1 will now equal 3. Each partner remains an individual while adding a potent new dimension: namely, the power to achieve commonality in one's life.

> The meeting of two personalities is like the contact of two chemical substances: if there is any reaction, both are transformed.
>
> CARL JUNG

The six images in the psyche of man and woman

In her book "Nature Seen in a Different Way", Doris Bischof-Köhler writes, "Even today, the view is constantly expressed that behavioral differences between genders are exclusively socio-culturally determined. If the sexes were to be treated equally, it is expected that there would be a corresponding leveling of such differences. This position, however, cannot be supported based on empirical evidence. If the goal is to explain gender differences adequately, there is no alternative but to include consideration of innate factors. The reason the sexes behave differently is grounded in their natural biological evolution." Such differences were also observed by Anne Moir and David Jessel: "The sexes are different because their brains are different. The brain, the chief administrative and emotional organ of life, is differently constructed in men and women; it processes information in a different way, which results in different perceptions, priorities, and behavior." They maintain that it is precisely these major differences between men and women that produce the fascination that the sexes exert on each other.

The basic lore regarding relationship success includes six images that are grounded in male psychology and female psychology. They constitute such a strong influence over partner selection and the development of a relationship that they leave little space for conscious decision-making. What sort of images are these?

The male archetype, the female archetype

Male and female archetypes originate in the animalistic unconscious. Such cases describe an archaic 'predator-prey' system based on past criteria used in selecting mates. This system dates to the Stone Age but continues to exert its subconscious influence on each of us.

Stefan Woinoff writes about this in his book "Expand Your Predator-Prey System": "In those times, a man's body size equated to his status for all practical purposes: a tall, powerful man enjoyed high status in the community, while women able to attract such a man enhanced the likelihood of ensuring the security of their children."

Men, on the other hand, responded to the archaic predator-prey system by being particularly attracted to women with hourglass figures. To men, such women gave off signals of fertility and a predilection for bearing children.

The subjective image based on individual conditioning

A man's mother is the first woman in his life, and a woman's father is the first man in her life. The subjective image of our mother and father that we formed in childhood affects the actual image of women and men we carry into corresponding experiences in the world.

The subjective ideal image

Based on inhibitions and shortcomings in one's own personality system, the subjective ideal image is formed almost as a complementary view. The stronger the inhibition and frustration, the stronger the ideal image will be inflated: at that point, we want to avail ourselves of one individual – our partner – to make up for everything that is missing in ourselves.

Since many people, in fact, only marry the ideal image of their partner, this becomes very difficult for the actual, existing partner. That person is always forced to take a back seat, is frequently seen as a flawed compromise, and is merely tolerated. In this way, a man can never do right by a woman who has elevated her father as her ideal, and a woman will never win the heart of a man who unconsciously continues to cling to his mother or idolizes an actress or model. The difficulty in all these cases lies in the fact that the ideal image leads to permanent criticism, berating, and devaluation of the real, existing partner. This frequently results in separation, since the partner does not match up to the ideal image.

All these behavior patterns, rooted in the ideal image, produce a considerable amount of illness, pain, and suffering. In many cases, potential partners are constantly rejected because of this ideal image, leading to a great dearth of love, tenderness, and sexuality in the world. Many individuals even prefer to remain single for many years rather than accept any compromise. They tell themselves, "The right partner for me has to exist somewhere in the world." They are convinced that there is a lid for every pot, a key for every lock. They often wait their entire lives for the right person and are filled with resentment over the partners in their past who did not live up to their ideal.

The image of the partner in sexual fantasy

The image of the partner in sexual fantasy usually differs from the ideal image that the unconscious has created as a counterbalance. The sexual fantasy partner does not necessarily have to go through life with you. One is an ideal image for life, the other an ideal image for the bed.

The partner in a sexual fantasy is the image that compensates for the inability to achieve satisfaction of one's own needs in the sexual arena and for all internal and external blockages that stand in the way of satisfaction. Many women wait their entire lives for the ideal partner (see point 3) and, as a result, reject potential partners or, for a variety of reasons (for example, an inner prohibition), do not have such a strong need for sexuality as is frequently the case with men. The resulting scarcity of actual sexual opportunities drives millions of men to seek out erotic images of women. Through the Internet and the constant availability of such images, this quest for erotic images can even become an addiction.

The image of the true partner in oneself

Within ourselves, each of us harbors our true partner.

The image of the true partner that we carry within us is the result of the individual unconscious: only we can be the true partner for ourselves!

This true partner in me is fundamentally different from the ideal image of the partner. The question of how I can be a good partner to myself is easily answered: by balancing myself. By developing and realizing in myself that which I would otherwise expect from my partner.

The subjective image of one's own partner

In this image, the partner is not perceived as he or she truly is. Above all, this perception results from the conditioning from the past, the subjective image of father and mother, and the ideal image of the partner that distorts one's own perspective in this way.

The situation is aggravated by the fact that every person produces different reactions and behavior patterns depending on the relationship. In this way, one woman can trigger the sensitive lover in a man while another awakens in him the habitual complainer.

Apart from the images that we create of our real, existing partner, this person evades our consciousness. A partner's true nature only becomes clear when we confront our own delusions that have been created by the different images.

A couple's path from the unconscious to the conscious

No man, when pledging himself to his bride at their wedding ceremony, thinks: "This woman will become my psychological trash dump -- I will destroy this woman." And no woman thinks, while murmuring "I do" at her wedding, "I will mentally castrate this man and turn him into a loser!"

Yet over time, despite the best intentions of both partners, their relationship increasingly generates disagreements, conflict and, ultimately, aggression and hate.

How is this possible? Why don't couples grow ever closer? Why can't they be successful in what nearly all partners want: becoming stronger together than on their own, functioning as a team, achieving more in life by working together, experiencing in tandem greater security, happiness, and zest for life?

Most couples believe that only their partner is at fault when the relationship fails. They reason, "My intentions were good, but my partner would not cooperate – it's just not possible to build a good relationship with such a person." To the question of how to develop such a successful relationship, very few can provide an answer.

In short: we generally know neither the real reason behind the breakdown of a relationship nor what a constructive relationship-building process looks like.

And how can we be expected to know these things when our own parents and grandparents almost never reflected on such matters, when no class on 'relationship skills' was offered in our schools, and, above all, when we show no concern for the unconscious although it governs our entire lives almost exclusively?

Let's just say it bluntly: two people who become a couple are usually at the mercy of all their unconscious mechanisms and programs. Most of these individuals are merely puppets of their unconscious – more specifically, their unconscious influences. Even so, they are firmly convinced that all their decisions and reactions are conscious ones. They are unaware that their unconscious is the director of their play as well as the author of the script for their partner relationship that has such an important role in determining the happiness and unhappiness in their lives. If these two people no longer wish to be unconscious actors in a film whose script they do not know, their only option is to deal with these unconscious influences and directives.

Doing so involves recognizing the effect exerted by father, mother, and siblings, the respective gender roles defined and expressed by parents, and the effects of environment, culture, and the age we live in. Important questions to be asked in clarifying these forces include: What roles was I pushed into, and who did my parents expect me to become? What traumas have I experienced? What psychological wounds and pains do I have? What tendencies do I unconsciously avoid so that I can maintain my pet emotions and my current life direction? When I was growing up, where were habits and life topics suppressed, made taboo, ignored, repressed, devalued, put on a pedestal, dogmatized, or glorified? What have I acquired from my parents? Where have I developed merely a response pattern, and where has a contrarian attitude or alternative stance emerged?

The environment in which the individual has been raised is also of great importance. There is a great deal of difference, for example, whether one comes from the lower class or the upper middle class. Every socioeconomic class has its own language, lifestyle, signals, and status symbols, its own patterns of emotions and thoughts, its own role-playing, its own ways of acting and behaving, and so forth.

For many people, the class-specific influence is so effective, occurring so imperceptibly, that throughout life these individuals create the deception that they have truly developed a different way of feeling, thinking, and acting. In fact, they are merely repeating the attitudes and opinions that predominate in the surrounding environment. Had a person belonged to a different social class, he or she would possibly have acted out an entirely different set of behaviors. Someone who displays rebellious characteristics would probably stand out in the lower class as defiant and resistant with respect to authority figures, while the same person in a more educated class would offer intellectual resistance, perhaps in the form of subversive ideas.

To avoid any misunderstanding: the ways of playing out one's individual resources are not determined solely by the cultural milieu but also through one's psychological and intellectual development. To belong to a higher social class is not always an advantage. For example, feelings are often expressed directly and bluntly in the lower class, and this tendency can be connected to a psychological cleansing process; whereas negative feelings such as aggression, hatred, or rage are less openly tolerated in other social classes and thus must find other outlets.

From all that has been described to this point, it is clear how important it is for both partners to recognize the forces, sabotage mechanisms, cravings for power, aggressions, inappropriate emotional patterns, and mistaken beliefs they harbor within themselves.

It should also be borne in mind that, at an unconscious level, every person follows his or her animal instincts. This means that behind the mask of culture is something completely different – possibly a turf-defending, sex-driven, power-hungry, intolerant, rude, rebellious, and fearful anarchist.

Since this is the case, it would be wise for a couple to take off their masks, which are only artificial façades, and face each other as they really are. Only in this way can they create intimacy and trust. Each of them can develop understanding for how the other has arrived at this point. The partners can support each other in exposing old behavior patterns and fallacious beliefs. By increasing their awareness of unconscious influences, they can assist their partner, engage their partner in discussion, and – after they have become more advanced in this awareness-building process – even laugh about some things that earlier would have snared them emotionally and left them in old entanglements.

Each one knows that the partner acts with good intentions toward the other, that true mutual benevolence exists, with each partner embracing the adventure of a lifetime. The pursuit of perfection diminishes, and it is no longer necessary to be right all the time, to constantly prove superiority over the other. Each partner confesses mistakes and shortcomings to the other and stops condemning the other's failings.

The couple becomes increasingly capable of having a birds-eye perspective on the relationship, examining and discussing situations as they arise. As Marshall B. Rosenberg, the founder of 'Nonviolent Communication', would view it, the conscious couple is finally able to communicate with each other.

At this point, many readers will argue that this could only be accomplished by two partners with psychology degrees. I would like to reject this interpretation: if both partners are honestly and sincerely ready to get to know each other and themselves, and if each of them is interested not only in continuing their relationship but in imbuing it with depth, intimacy, and trust, they can travel this path, growing psychologically and intellectually as individuals and as a couple.

The path leads from the unconscious couple, subject almost totally to unconscious pursuits, to the conscious couple that shows understanding for the unconscious mechanisms and achieves a mutual awareness of these.

The conscious couple lives according to the saying of the Persian poet Hafiz:

> If each one knew everything about the other, forgiveness of the other would be easy, there would be no more pride, no arrogance.

Questions for reflection concerning the unconscious

- Where did my last relationship fall apart?
- Have I developed an idea of how I can contribute to building a constructive relationship?
- Do I allow the animal in me to live? Or do I try everything to suppress and repress it?
- How much am I governed by the collective unconscious?
- Am I aware of my unconscious life plan (my script) and my screenplay?
- What role do I play in this screenplay, and what role does my partner play?
- Is it possible for me to view the stage play of my life from a birds-eye perspective?
- When I do this, can I recognize my drama, soap opera, comedy, or tragedy?
- When I do this, do I see how different it is from reality?
- What awareness of life's eternal truths have I gained so far?
- Am I ready to carry out a process of individuation and in this way distinguish myself from the norm?
- Is my partner ready to accompany me on the path from the unconscious to the conscious?
- Am I only married to an ideal image of my partner?
- Do I see the real, existing partner at my side as he or she really is?

PART TWO
Becoming aware of inner conflicts

When your life is dark, look to see if it is because all your window shutters are closed.
JOHANNES KEPLER

The right partner is an illusion

Millions of people wait for the 'right' partner. They hope one day to be rewarded by destiny and, through miraculous providence, encounter that one individual who is their ideal image of a partner. Indeed, many even pray to God that he send them Mr./Ms. Right. They firmly believe that someone exists with whom they can be happy to the end of their days. They have a precise idea as to how this ideal partner should look, how the partner should feel and think, what sort of education he or she should have, what leisure interests, and so on. They dream of being able to say, "That is my husband!" or "that is my wife!" They are intimately acquainted and completely in agreement with this person. This is their other half, so to speak: their opposite-sex counterpart, their kindred spirit.

While it all sounds beautiful, this inner ideal partner who accompanies us everywhere can in fact create negative consequences for the individual as well as for all potential partners. This can lead to:

- devaluation of other people by comparing them to their ideal image. For example, women reject men because they do not stand up under comparison with their inner ideal partner. In those being rejected, this frequently produces feelings of worthlessness, pain, sadness, and anger.
- the development of arrogance, since they believe that their own high standards are evidence that they have attained a higher level than have their prospective partners. They do not see the need to compromise those standards.
- loneliness, both within themselves and when they are with potential partners.
- a tendency, when they condescend to attach themselves to someone who does not meet the criteria of the ideal partner,

to criticize or lash out at this person. They usually want to change or remake the individual to become their ideal partner over time.

- loss of a valuable portion of their lives as they wait for Mr. or Ms. Right, denying themselves – as well as the potential partner – enjoyable hours of tenderness and love.
- fear that, by contenting themselves with someone who falls short of their ideal partner, they will no longer be available when Mr. or Ms. Right ascends the stage of their life.
- rejection (based on the ideal image) of developmental steps that would be important to their own character.
- all types of compulsive behaviors. These serve as compensation for the frustration that they are with the wrong partner and that Mr. or Ms. Right has not yet appeared.

Instead of getting at the true cause of their actual situation, they merely continue their frenzied search in the fog for Mr. or Ms. Right.

The following ten points should demonstrate why the idea of the dream partner is nothing more than an illusion. There can be no 'right' partner so long as we...

1. ... do not know who we are, while the Delphic maxim "know thyself" remains unfulfilled.
2. ... are unable to recognize who our partner is, and so long as our partner likewise does not know who he or she is.
3. ... fail to realize that the world is bipolar, that in some areas, we need an opposite-pole partner to achieve balance; for example, a cleanliness fanatic needs a messy partner. In that sense, the 'wrong' partner can also be 'right' (this is explained in detail in Part Four).
4. ... fail to understand that a relationship built on the illusion of the dream partner is only 'right' if neither partner continues to develop. Even just one partner's further development is usually enough to undermine the entire relationship.
5. ... are unable to recognize that the relationship is instantly over when one partner refuses to fulfill the other's role assignments or to continue performing in the other's biographical film or stage play, or if the partner does not play by the established rules of the game.
6. ... do not know that a relationship usually breaks up if the

man reveals his sexual fantasies.

7. ... cannot accept that the partner is a distinct individual who cannot be possessed – in other words, who does not belong to the other partner. In this respect, jealousy, and all efforts to control and monitor the partner are unwarranted.
8. ... refuse to acknowledge that, to survive in our civilization, every human being creates a façade or cultural mask that contrasts with his or her animal nature. Most of us have either pushed into our unconscious or projected onto others everything that is incompatible with our own positive self-image or our own ideal ego. In doing so, we want to have nothing to do with all this. Amazingly, many individuals are confident that they are truly as they appear. In addition, they regard the façades created by others as the true nature of those individuals. Yet behind the cultural mask lurk many negative feelings that we attempt with all our power to suppress but that continue to break through: aggression, rivalry, egoism, greed, territoriality, envy, hate, boasting, lustfulness, ambition, obstruction, rebellion, superiority, and fear. Thus, in a partner relationship, one mask is often merely placed on another. It usually takes us years or even decades to discover who is hiding behind these masks. Let's state it bluntly: a successful relationship always involves coming to know the partner's animal nature. And this requires assertiveness and, above all, courage.
9. ... refuse to admit that everyone, even someone in a permanent relationship, has a need for opportunities with the opposite sex.
10. ... are unaware that most of us are so strongly influenced by fashion and mainstream thought that these ideas play a crucial role in our choice of a partner – in other words, that we are always attracted to that which is 'in' at that specific time and place.

Thus, it is almost never apparent to us whether this partner is in fact a good fit behind all the masks, roles, passing fashions, and mainstream conventions – in other words, in the person's true nature. Moreover, the discrepancy between the conscious and the unconscious has an effect. The partner may fit with the unconscious but not with the conscious (or vice versa). This all reveals that even if the partner is seemingly a good match, no lasting fulfillment is possible.

In sum: the right partner must remain an illusion because it is not the conscious but the unconscious that governs the partner relationship. That is where there is indeed a 'right' partner, although this is often entirely different from what our conscious sees as right.

It can therefore be said: only a very specific partner is able to make the other aware of what is suppressed, unconscious and unresolved. To do this requires the partner to master specific learning processes that are important to the other and that advance his or her self-development.

If the essence is not changed, nothing essential is changed.

The woman's internal team

Twelve archetypal beings inhabit the psyche of every woman, forming a team. Each woman carries these internal family members and coworkers within herself. A woman can activate any of the following subpersonalities:

1. Initiator (active supporter)
2. Pleasure-seeker
3. Intellectual (informant)
4. Mother (caregiver, tender
5. Manager (organizer)
6. Healer (analyst)
7. Erotic seductress (lover, mistress)
8. Sexually active woman
9. Partner (i.e., wife)
10. Muse (inspiration)
11. Lady
12. Amazon

An effective team results when all twelve subpersonalities work together – meaning that the woman can play all her trump cards for the benefit of her personal well-being and that of her children and partner. In this way, an interesting and joyful life is open to her.

It is more difficult, however, if certain subpersonalities are not activated and trained or if they do not act in a coordinated fashion or possibly even work against one another.

While seven of these subpersonalities – initiator, pleasure-seeker, intellectual, manager, healer, lady, and Amazon – are essential for independent living, above all it is the other five subpersonalities – mother, erotic seductress, sexually active woman, partner, and muse – that are crucial if a partner relationship is to be successful.

In the "Sources of Happiness" chapter we will explore the important roles played by these five subpersonalities in pleasure, tenderness, eroticism, sexuality, mutual caring, and emotional development. For the development of awareness and the resolution of inner conflicts, however, it is first necessary to reflect on the physical mother, inner mother, and true mother within a person.

These, then, are the three mothers:

1. My real, existing mother as she once was and as she is today.
2. My own inner mother and my own inner mother image: in other words, the way my mother affected me during childhood and how I reacted to her. As a small child whose judgment was not yet formed and who was still incapable of objectivity, how did I feel and experience this mother? Based on that, what mother image inhabits my psyche? What emotional patterns and beliefs of mine have resulted from her influence on me? To what extent have these influences affected my feelings and thoughts today and determined my attraction to partners and the course of my relationships?
3. The true mother in oneself is referred to as the archetypal mother. Every person carries her within, and she simply embodies what is motherly and feminine – as principle, potential, capacity, and quality. This is the primal image of the feminine that lives within each woman and man.

Based on the enormous importance for one's psychic life, the following section describes the path from one's own inner mother to the true mother within oneself in the form of a statement and in a sort of affirmation. This affirmation is especially significant for those who experienced a difficult relationship with their mothers.

This path involves breaking free from the influence of the personal unconscious – from all the mistaken beliefs and response patterns that make our life unnecessarily difficult.

My physical mother

My physical mother is the external representative of an internal archetype. She has sought to embody this true motherly principle at her level of development and awareness. Since no one is perfect, she sometimes expressed this in an inadequate or distorted way. She had good intentions, but she was usually unaware of the consequences of what she had done, since she did not know the laws of life and destiny.

I am grateful to my mother because she gave birth to me, raised me, cared for me rather well, and devoted a large part of her life to me.

I respect my mother and visit her from time to time, but I do not allow her to continue to influence me and my life. I take care not to fall back into old behaviors and not to use the old response patterns in my contacts with her. I do not blame my mother for what she has done wrong and for all that I have not received from her.

For the crucial thing is that my mother serves as the trailblazer to my true inner mother. Based on the true mother in me, I can free myself from my physical mother and from her related influence. Fully at ease, I can let go and finally cut my umbilical cord. When I can discover my true mother as a valuable resource within me, when I can experience her myself, I will at last have truly grown up. I can accept myself and will no longer unconsciously or consciously seek my physical mother's acceptance or praise.

The true mother within me

Many capabilities and qualities are bound up in the true mother within an individual. These primarily are the result of Mother Nature. What all is contained here?

The Mother Nature in me

The Mother of human nature in me

The Mother of feminine nature in me

The archetype of the feminine in me

The true woman in me

The caregiver in me (for myself)

My world of feelings

My inner state of mind

My true nature

My psychological identity

My true dwelling within myself

My inner home

My inner security

The psychological love within me and for me

The intimacy with me

The psychological warmth for me

The voice of life within me

The access to my true needs

The nourishment that is right for me

Self-acceptance

All these are manifestations and nuances of the same principle. To experience these qualities in oneself is something exquisite and wonderful, something that subtly engenders happiness. And the beautiful thing is: in this way, you are dependent upon no one, everything rests in your own hands. To experience the true mother and the qualities bound up in her signifies the following:

I see to it myself that things go well for me (I take care of my own well-being)

I am a good mother to myself (and *therefore* also a good mother for my family)

I gain access to my physical, psychological, and intellectual needs and fulfill them

I have access to my emotional life

I develop my own sex life (I know myself)

I have access to the voice of life within me

I discover the true woman in me and allow her to grow and live

I discover the proper nutrition for me

I discover my inner child

I am secure in myself

I have psychological warmth and love for myself

I have inner contentment (my needs are satisfied)

I enjoy healthy sleep

At heart, all this only means that we understand what has to be done: we must learn to accept and affirm ourselves if we hope to be accepted and affirmed by others; we must be a good mother to ourselves to be able to be a good mother to others; we must become intimate with ourselves before we can achieve intimacy with our partner; we must feel secure in ourselves before we can feel secure with our partner; and we must see that our own needs are met before we can expect that our partner will meet our needs.

You cannot escape yourself.
GOETHE

The dysfunctional father relationship

This chapter examines the fateful repercussions a woman must face if her relationship to her father was impaired or if she has an outsized positive relationship with her father.

If a woman had a dysfunctional and difficult father relationship, possibly because the father was conspicuous in his absence, constantly authoritative in his control, or otherwise derelict in his behavior, the chances are good that many of her relationships with men will fail.

She cannot respect or acknowledge any man, let alone love him for his true qualities, because she sees only similarly negative qualities in her partner based on her unconscious father transference. She focuses on the man's weak points and on his negative side for the purpose of repeating and reliving the old emotional patterns, reaction modes and beliefs. Because of these, she cannot perceive any partner in his true essence. Exactly the opposite! In each case, she is linked only to a phantom partner – that is, to the illusion of a partner that is at odds with the evidence.

Sometimes she attracts partners who in fact display some similarities to her father, confirming her feelings and thoughts that men are bad, evil, or flawed. It is no wonder, therefore, when her relationships follow an inauspicious course like that with her own father.

In a high proportion of women with a dysfunctional father relationship, an antithetical image of the father takes shape – first in the unconscious, then in her conscious. For example: if her father was a patriarch, this evokes the mental counter-image of a pliant, docile, and subservient man. What she does not know is that this image will turn her into a feminine patriarch and lead her to project onto her partner the pole that she personified as a weak little girl.

When the man appears 'in her film', she becomes bewildered and unable to perceive reality. Usually, she has in mind a host of role assignments for him to fulfill if he is to qualify as a good man in her eyes, and she lays down precise rules of the game regarding his behavior. If the partner in this 'counter-image film' fails to play along, or if he does not play his role precisely enough, a tendency to devalue him soon emerges. At that point, he is attacked and insulted because he does not exactly fit the counter-image of her father. This is known as a counter-image fixation.

How can a woman affected in this way resolve this dilemma? This can be achieved if she becomes conscious of all this and, in the end – as we shall see further on – finds her true father in herself.

Father-identification and the Electra complex

We have become familiar with the issues related to women whose relationship to their own father is impaired. Some men, as a result, conclude that it would be better to become involved with a woman who has had a very good father relationship. In this way, one might assume, the man would also fare very well when that relationship is transferred to him. But such an assumption is far off the mark! He often fares much worse! How can that be possible?

Let's look at the case of Simone, the only child of prosperous parents. She had a poor relationship to her mother but a particularly good one with her father. She admired her father, who, in his career, reached the highest rungs of the company hierarchy seemingly without effort. As a child, she was sometimes allowed to go to work with her father, where two women in the reception area cared for her affectionately. Wherever she went with him, the employees were kind and polite to her, and she could perceive the influence and power her father wielded. She only moved out of her parents' house and into her own residence at age 31. She continued her close connection to her father, however. She went on weekend outings with him, played golf at his club, and consulted him whenever she had a problem.

With Simone, the issue appears to be an Electra complex that she has not overcome.[*] This is reflected in the daughter's love for her father and concurrent aversion to her mother. This caused Simone to have continual difficulties with men. Her greatest wish was to have a child but, as she often said, all the men she encountered were only a 50 to 60 percent match with her, and she did not want to risk a relationship with any of them. Above all, none could be compared to her father.

It is clear by this point that Simone had not yet accomplished the process of detaching herself from her father. She was always his 'princess' and there was no room in her unconscious that could accommodate a partner. She was in fact 'married' to her father, and the real, flesh-and-blood men who trod the stage of her life never had a chance. For the same reason, women like Simone rarely have children, since they unconsciously want to remain 'daddy's little girl': they do not want to bring their own competitor into the world. This phenomenon is frequently the cause of childlessness.

A further issue is that, because her father played his role so well, she developed an unrealistic concept of the masculine principle. After all, she never experienced her father as husband and lover, seeing him only from the perspective of a daughter – or a 'princess.'

She had no knowledge of his other, possibly secret life and was unaware of his repression and dark sides. She could not perceive that she knew only the role he played as her father but not the man hiding behind that role. For this reason, she also had no realistic approach to sexuality. She suffered from a commitment disorder and had difficulty achieving orgasm (see also the chapters on bound-up energies and on commitment disorder and orgasm roadblocks as consequences of unconscious fears of relationships).

Let us return once again to the portrayal of the father's role. Many parents act out a role for their children (for example, they model tolerance, benevolence, courtesy, decency, seriousness, etc.). In this way, once the children become adults, they have no knowledge of what kind of people their parents truly were. A false father or mother image has developed and, along with it, a false image of men or women. The children usually never experience what reality was and is.

The consequences of a negative or positive father image for a man

Accordingly, an impaired father relationship is a pivotal matter for a woman. Does such a relationship also lead to adverse consequences in the life of a man?

It has been repeatedly shown that men who are in constant disagreement with their father or who hate their father unconsciously incur a host of problems. For one, if they were confronted with an authoritarian father as a child, they feel themselves drawn to persons of authority as a means of repeating and continuing the negative experiences with their father (unconscious repetition compulsion). This even goes as far as developing bad experiences with people who share the same job as their father or have one like it. Other consequences of an impaired father relationship may be resignation, retreat from the world, or even a tendency to self-neglect, but they may also include opposite reactions, such as an enormous ambition to outperform their father. The individual wants (usually unconsciously) to demonstrate that he is better than his father, that he earns more, owns a better house, has more influential friends ... Even if the son has long since surpassed his father, his striving usually has no end for him. He is driven from within to go farther and farther without ceasing, like Sisyphus and his labors.

But what does this mean for the selection of a partner? A man can also experience his flawed father relation in situations with women, since transference is fundamentally sex-independent. In this sense, even a feminine partner can exhibit certain fatherly traits. The individual has the sensation of reliving the same hell he previously went through with his father. The ambience that prevailed back then once again hangs in the air.

But shouldn't things go better if a man has a good father relationship?

In such a case, a different problem frequently emerges: the man walks too deliberately in his father's footsteps, finding it very difficult to discover his own identity or completely transferring patterns of feeling, thinking, and acting, possibly choosing the same political party, driving the same brand of car, or practicing the same sport. It can be even worse if he has such total admiration for his father that he remains forever the little boy who cannot keep pace with his father and whose achievements can never equal his father's. In some cases, even as a grown man, he is forced to ask his father for material or moral support.

But – if neither a negative nor a positive father image contributes to one's own destiny, what would a solution look like? It is basically quite simple: what works the best has always been, and continues to be, a realistic father image.

This means achieving inner separation from the old father image. Over time, this results in a man no longer having inhibitions and blockages when taking actions and in putting ideas into practice; no longer does he allow excessive ambition to encroach on his quality of life, acting instead in a proper and responsible manner because he has become a responsible father to himself and others. He manages his own life in such a way that everything is sorted out, all subpersonalities are permitted to live, and his own life can find expression. For this to occur, however, it is necessary that he find the true father in himself.

Transference of a good or bad father or mother relationship

At this point, let us return to the aspect of the unconscious transference to persons of authority. Transference and countertransference are terms used to describe phenomena that are familiar in psychoanalysis. During treatment, the patient develops an emotional response to the therapist, identifying the therapist with a person who once played a key role in an early emotional conflict. This phase of therapy is called transference. In most cases, the analyst is identified with a parent. Transference is deemed positive if the feelings toward the therapist are affectionate or admiring; it is negative if filled with hostility, resentment, or envy. A patient's attitude can frequently be ambivalent: he or she can have both positive and negative feelings toward the therapist, just as children frequently do toward their parents. Since it can be difficult for the analyst always to respond to the patient in an emotionally neutral way, a so-called countertransference can take place. Here, based on a perceived similarity between the patient and a significant person in the therapist's own life, the therapist develops positive or negative feelings toward the patient.

Such transference and countertransference occur not just in psychotherapy but in daily life as well. This unconscious process consists of transferring past attitudes, feelings, and expectations to another person: the emotional causes of transference are to be found not in the present situation but in earlier life circumstances, usually from early childhood. The current situation, the actual person occupying life's stage, serves as the key stimulus and projection surface. In this way, the interpersonal situation or conflict is perceived in merely a restricted and distorted manner. The person responding to such an offer of transference (such a response is called partner attraction or resonance) yields to countertransference.

In this manner, father, mother, grandmother, grandfather, brother, sister, or other early figures of attachment can, through *transference*, once again make an appearance in one's life as (spousal) partner, boy- or girlfriend, boss, fellow worker, or even one's own child.

Based on this unconscious transference mechanism, a man who has experienced an impaired father relationship can develop a tendency to become close to father figures or persons of authority who then cause problems for him. This can occur either because the relationship is truly prejudicial or because he projects bad things onto it so that he can once again experience the earlier situation.

A healthy or impaired mother relationship does not unfold differently than a good or bad father relationship. An intact mother relationship makes it easier to have good subsequent experiences with women, while in a poor mother relationship, the adult man frequently surrounds himself with moralists, emotional blackmailers, rivals, backstabbers, and schemers.

For those who suffer from a difficult father or mother relationship, the best solution to this adverse transference mechanism is to find one's true mother and true father in oneself. The chapters "*The True Mother in Me*" and "*The True Father in Me*" describe how to achieve success in this effort. Experience has shown that interpersonal contacts and relationships can subsequently be improved in a very short time in many cases.

> *If you bring forth what is in you, that which you bring forth or express will heal you.*
> *If you do not bring forth what is in you, that which you do not bring forth can destroy you.*
> ANONYMOUS

The man's internal team

As for women, the man's internal team is made up of twelve players, each of which portrays an archetypal person. These archetypes or subpersonalities need to work in harmony to achieve victory in the game of life. Each of these must contribute its talents and capabilities in the service of the whole. In doing so, who acts where and when is of great importance. Only when the right player occupies the right place and knows his task, only when his timing is right, does it become possible for a man to become – and remain – a successful person. Here is the lineup:

1. Hero (victor, pioneer, active supporter)
2. Pleasure-seeker (territory defender)
3. Informant (intellectual)
4. Tender lover (cuddle bear)
5. Father (manager, doer)
6. Critic (analyst)
7. Erotic seducer
8. Sexually active man
9. Partner (husband)
10. Savant (intellectual inspiration)
11. Gentleman
12. Renovator (independent, idea generator, future designer)

Becoming a father is easy enough, but being one can be very rough.
WILHELM BUSCH

My physical father

If a man has a good team supporting him, he feels happy and strong. He can design his life on his own, can reach fulfillment without assistance, is less dependent. He finds gratification in his love relationships when he has his cuddle bear, erotic seducer, sexually active man, partner (caregiver) and savant subpersonalities on the field.

Before describing the resources and capacities of the paternal principle, it is first necessary to provide a few thoughts regarding one's own physical father and the true father in oneself. As with the physical mother, this is best done in the form of a statement or affirmation.

My physical father did everything he could to act as the representative of an inner archetype. His cultural milieu, times, and personal circumstances prevented a better and more perfect portrayal. I am grateful to my father that he raised me and that he took care of me and wanted to take care of me, that he devoted time to me and protected me.

In the end, however, he was merely the trailblazer for my true inner father. When I discover and experience this father within me, I will have grown up. Once I have trained and developed my true father's resources and capacities, my physical father will no longer be meaningful. I will then have accomplished the process of separation from him. This is as true for me as a woman with an impaired father relationship and electra complex as it is for me as a man with a flawed or healthy father relationship.

I no longer want (unconsciously) to do right by him, no longer constantly react to him (trained response patterns of which one is only rarely truly conscious). I no longer need his recognition, but neither must I remain generally at odds with him (or, through transference, with my boss, fellow workers, or partner). I have become the manager of my life and I fulfill myself. I protect myself against injury and harm directed against me. I am the author of my actions and creations, and my inner creative spirit is endowed with inexhaustible potential.

The true father within me

As of now, my true father within me will replace my physical father in marking a new point of reference in my life. The following should explain what distinguishes this inner father and what systems and capacities are ingrained in him.

The true father within me
The creative spirit within me
My inner self
The manager of my life within me
The boss within me
The provider within me
The true man within me
The actualizer within me
The designer within me
The entrepreneur within me
The protector within me
The supporter within me (supporting myself)
The light source within me
My self-awareness
The ability to act within me
The constructiveness within me
The autonomy within me
My emotional security
My sense of humor
The good will for me

The man who becomes his own father for himself will step back from continual blame of his physical father for the grievances and difficulties in his own life. The father is not responsible for these; up to this point, the man himself has only borne the responsibility of activating and experiencing his own father within himself.

Seen from a purely chronological perspective, the first and most important priority is to activate the mother within us. This is because she represents our emotional identity. We must get to know her if we want to fend for ourselves and discover our true needs. Only then will it be possible to activate the inner father, who then acts in accordance with our own identity and our own true feelings and thus seeks to express these qualities.

This is because otherwise we are not acting in accordance with our own identity, and consequently all actions, undertakings and realizations are carried out to no avail – meaning here that all these actions fail to satisfy us. This happens because we cannot achieve what is in accordance with our first nature, but instead only its substitute, which ultimately cannot bring about our fulfillment.

Taking steps to develop the connection to our true mother and true father within us is of crucial significance to the partner relationship. This action is prerequisite to our being able to extinguish all the old physical, psychological, and intellectual patterns of responding to our parents so that we may lead an independent and autonomous life as an adult. In so doing, it becomes possible for us to build a constructive relationship based on reality. While in the past our relationship usually worsened through the years due to old wounds and our unconscious, infantile, conflict-producing behavior patterns, now it continually improves as we become aware of our inner mother and inner father and actualize their qualities.

A truly great man will neither trample on a worm nor sneak to an emperor.
BENJAMIN FRANKLIN

From little man to alpha male

In his heart and soul, every man really wants to be the leader of the pack and an alpha male. But only a very few manage to rise to that status.

While in the old days a real man was a hero whose strength and power distinguished him from other men, or a hunter who was exceptionally skilled, today we particularly admire the one who is more successful than the others in climbing to the top or using his ingenuity to acquire the financial means to ensure a better standard of living for his family.

Specifically, due to his animal programming and traditional understanding of roles, he must be able to support his family. This is usually quite easy for him if he manages to advance beyond subordinate positions and become the leader. To accomplish this, he must develop ambition, learn, stay informed, continue his education, attend success and management seminars, perform, elbow his way to the front, assert himself, and eliminate his rivals.

Almost every man would like to achieve a leadership position, be in charge, change the instructions, tell others how it is going to be, have a staggering intellect and, at a minimum, make manager in his company or, if possible, rise further to senior manager, director, general director, or big boss. One reason for such aspirations, moreover, is to maximize his chances with the opposite sex. According to a study by the Düsseldorf motivational research institute Ives Marketing, 98 percent of men between 26 and 35 indicated that success in their career was their greatest ambition. A psychoanalytical survey revealed that the purpose of their desires for professional achievement was to have better success with women. Men strive for professional success, therefore, to gain an edge in the battle to conquest a sexual partner, to develop an allure that will make them appear more attractive to women.

What does a man need to feel good about himself?

- He wants to be the boss/be professionally successful
- He wants to do (pursue) business (i.e., make financial gains)
- He wants to be a winner in sports
- He wants to be a favorite with the ladies

- He wants to have a house or a condominium
- He wants to be able to provide high-quality sustenance
- He wants to drive a car that matches his status

It is possible for him to stabilize his personality system along all these factors. There are men who possess the ability to do well in one or two of these areas, but only a few succeed in all of them.

The above points represent fundamental avenues for compensation in maintaining one's own health as a man. It is possible to speak of **male psychosomatics**: the more fields available to a man for him to distinguish himself, the less susceptible he is to illness – except of course for genetic disorders and predispositions to disease that result from compulsive behaviors or unhealthy lifestyles.

The weighting of the individual fields also plays a role in men's health. The entire personality system's susceptibility to breakdown is oriented to this sort of prioritization. Thus, some men become imbalanced and ill when their car malfunctions.

In other words, if one primary compensation level is absent because success in this area is no longer being achieved, the stability of the personality system is at risk. Where the corresponding area of life holds less significance for a man, however, he can continue to enjoy good health.

This also explains exactly why so many men fall ill when they retire: the move into retirement is accompanied by the loss of important compensation fields, and this energy, if it cannot be directed elsewhere, will end up being focused on the man himself.

What qualities, moreover, does an alpha male display? How can such a man be identified? Below are additional qualities that distinguish a true alpha male:

- An alpha male is educated, whether through academics or self-taught
- He is inventive-creative and imaginative, possessing mental virtuosity
- He provides his wife and children with support, safety, and security
- He conducts himself appropriately, has good manners
- He is communicative, drawing on comprehensive knowledge and background information
- He is distinguished by his ability to deal with conflict and can

identify solutions to conflicts
- He marches to his own drummer and pursues his own goals
- He is open to criticism and capable of assuming responsibility, i.e., he takes responsibility for his health, security and future and for environmental repercussions

Most of the time, it is not at all easy to identify a true alpha male in the real world. This is because there are a great many pseudo-alpha males or would-be alpha males: men who only simulate their alpha male status to those around them.

On the other hand, there are men who possess all the resources and capacities of an alpha male but who cannot be recognized as such, either because they themselves do not perceive their own capacities and resources or because they live in an environment where they are unable to give expression to these. Should it even become possible for such a man to perceive his alpha status, it remains in doubt whether the people surrounding him are also willing to acknowledge this status or whether he can maintain his position over time against rivals.

And one additional factor must not be overlooked: whether a man can assume the role of alpha male frequently depends on the zeitgeist. Appearance, behavior, some capabilities, or some talents are only in demand for a specific period. Before and after this time, the man who possess this quality will not achieve success.

I know that this life, missing its ripeness in love, is not altogether lost.
I know that the flowers that fade in the dawn the streams that strayed in the desert, are not altogether lost.
I know that whatever lags behind in this life laden with slowness is not altogether lost.
I know that my dreams that are still unfulfilled, and my melodies still unstruck, are clinging to some lute-strings of thine, and they are not altogether lost.
RABINDRANATH TAGORE

Female psychosomatics

There is a great difference between self-knowledge and self-actualization. While self-knowledge serves to promote awareness of repressed potential and to get to know one's own subpersonalities and their cross-linkages, self-actualization signifies shedding light on a resource, allowing it to live.

Those who do not illuminate their potential or energy are forced to suffer. Suffering refers to life energy directed against the person himself or herself. Life and pleasure become corrupted into pain and suffering. Thus, when, someone speaks of being in pain, this frequently equates to the person's not being sufficiently able to develop his or her talents and opportunities. Recovery thus depends in the first instance upon how successfully one can gradually shift one's own potential from the repression side, which constitutes a breeding ground for many different illnesses and conditions, to life's sunny side, to the side of fulfillment. The sick person must pose the question: for what need, for what idea, for what desire, for what dream, for what creation (child, picture, book, song, etc.), for what project is my illness a substitute? When we trace the causal chain back far enough, disease can be identified as the consequence of an unfulfilled need, a vocation not pursued, a repressed desire for a hobby, or a sport not taken up – in short, as the outcome of an unresolved situation calling attention to itself.

In this way, Ella contracted an ovarian cyst because the fulfillment of her desire for a child was frustrated by her family's financial stresses; Ramona developed chronic bronchitis due to her inability to quiet her urge to go clubbing after three years of marriage; Tobias contracted heart inflammation because he could not carry out an intensely hoped-for project.

In these cases, a resource is striving for the light but is blocked by inaccurate beliefs, standards, or ideals, by systemic deficiencies, or by a shortage of energy and assertiveness.

Fulfillment means redeeming one's life from its repressed, sick condition.

Despite increased empowerment, many women still have difficulties in achieving their vision of how they wish to live as a woman, especially where this vision is contrary to mainstream thinking.

It can happen, therefore, that a woman becomes ill because she is unable to experience that which makes her a woman and would give her pleasure, or because what the resources of her personality have so far been able to stabilize is now breaking down. The latter can occur if, for example, there are problems with her children, if her children grow up and leave home, if relational conflicts weigh her down, or if she is exposed to intrigues and harassment at work, if she can no longer experience something (such as social engagements, travel, friendships).

For all these reasons, it is extremely important for women to have the courage to articulate everything in her life that is incoherent or unharmonious and to ensure that she balances these in various ways (see the chapter "*Change Begins with Us*").

It is easy in the world to live after the world's opinion; it is easy in solitude to live after our own; but the great man is he who in the midst of the crowd keeps with perfect sweetness the independence of solitude.
RALPH WALDO EMERSON

Role assignments in the partner relationship

These days, having gone from the period of traditional role division to women's emancipation, couples are free to face the challenge of redefining their roles. Based upon the progressive individuation process and the rising expectations that accompany it, specific new role assignments have arisen that did not exist to this extent in earlier times. Whether we want to or not, each of us is compelled to play a variety of roles in our lives:

- Expected roles (for example, as assistant)
- Expected gender roles
- Expected sex roles
- Expected societal roles (for example, as professor or notary)
- Roles that require us to lie (roles that go against our true nature)
- Roles of which we are unaware
- Roles that are acquired or into which we are forced (for example, the role of a grumbler when we do not agree with a decision)
- Roles that we impose on others because of our own screenplay
- Roles that correspond to us
- Contradictory roles
- Dormant roles (for example, in marriage – with a different partner, other roles would be called for)

Due to a variety of deficiencies and needs, almost everyone tends to assign a role to his or her partner. This role is intended to balance our own shortcomings and address our needs. This does not pose any difficulties by itself. The problem is caused, however, by the fact that such role assigning usually takes place in a concealed and initially imperceptible way rather than out in the open.

Thus, the vision slumbering in the unconscious of our partner is not simply of us but also of the role we are expected to play in his or her biographical film.

Then, likewise in an unconscious manner, we employ our own conception of a partner and the attached partner roles when we choose from the various potential partners available to us. The only partner worth our consideration is the one we imagine could fill the role in our own biographical film. We believe that this is our only chance to achieve balance and contentment – i.e., to put our own world in order.

Since everyone has been forced into certain roles as a child – such as pretty boy, black sheep, slave, clown, prince, or princess, most of us are already accustomed to having to play a role. We learned at an early age that our life within our family was safeguarded by this function, and therefore we unconsciously hope that we will be loved by a partner who willingly performs his or her assigned role.

In a partner relationship, a struggle frequently emerges between the role assigners: each partner attempts to assign the other the role in the partner's biographical film.

Women primarily create screenplays and roles for the man that clearly prescribe what and how he should do in their life together and how he should show her that he is the man for whom she has yearned. Men, on the other hand, usually have very specific conceptions of how a woman should show him her femininity, what this femininity should look like, and what erotic and sexual behaviors she should exhibit.

We speak of gender-specific roles in such cases. They include:

- Role assignments that are linked to total self-denial and for this reason are unrealistic for virtually any partner. Such a role will probably not be gladly accepted by anyone.
- Roles that are so filled with contradictions that they cannot be enacted in real life.
- Role assignments that can only be fulfilled by very few partners whose sense of self-worth is
- Role assignments that some partners can take on without incurring very much psychological pain.
- Role assignments that were 'tailor-made' for some partners and that can therefore be easily fulfilled by them. Such a match is wonderful but rare: these individuals can live their own lives while still meeting their partner's role expectations.

To illustrate: the role assignment of a partner can be compared with a clearly defined job description in a career. It is possible that a man could imagine himself fully ready for a position as department head when in fact he possesses neither the technical requirements nor the necessary social competence or sufficient leadership qualities for the job.

The same applies to role assignments in a partner relationship. It is common for us to believe we can fulfill a role 'as written' and then find shortly after taking on this role that we fail completely in its execution. For example, someone with a middle-class income would like to fulfill the role his loved one expects of him as a man of the upper class and patron of the arts. In extreme cases, such an individual may even be tempted into criminal actions such as embezzlement or fraud just to impress the woman and fulfill or maintain the role assigned to him.

Most roles that we expect of our partner are unattainable or possibly attainable for only a short period of time. This is because roles that demand a great deal of self-denial do not survive in the long term. But a role can also be unattainable due to:

- many contradictions contained within the role assignment
- erroneous conceptions and beliefs – for example, that a highly intellectual partner can be distinguished by his or her expensive wristwatch or designer fashions.
- a false assumption that the partner will take pleasure in the same things that give us pleasure – i.e., that he or she will happily and eagerly fulfill the assigned role.
- an opposite-gender partner setting other life priorities and developing other interests based on a different hormonal balance.
- a partner having been raised in a different way and thus exhibiting a completely different personality, unable to live as we would like.

The basic problem inherent in role allocation in a romantic relationship is essentially always the same: those who expect a partner to correspond only to a role of their choosing are sending a signal that they do not want to know the person with whom they are joined.

Their message is: "I do not see all your wonderful assets and skills, I do not see your material, physical, emotional and intellectual resources. I do not see all the opportunities and potential open to me through you. In fact, even if you were a genius or one of the best partners in the world, I would not see that because I am only focused on the role I want you to play."

It often happens that the role we choose for our partner is impossible even if our partner is willing to play this role. If, for instance, a woman believes that her partner should spend every weekend on hikes in the mountains with her and her friends, it may turn out that such activities are not at all as pleasant and fulfilling as she imagined. This could be because her friends are unable to accept her new partner, or he seems out of place in such settings, or perhaps one of her girlfriends is flirting with him. Commonly the role takes on its own dynamic in such a situation and the continued enactment of the role is linked to psychological pain.

Although only the negative consequences of mutual role allocation have been described up to this point, it is important to note that most people are convinced that the role they assign to their partner has a positive effect, both for themselves and for the partner. This is rarely the case, however, since, as the mountain hiking example mentioned above makes clear, the action is frequently characterized by an inconsistency between concept and reality. Role allocations thus can often lead to dissatisfaction in the relationship and with the partner. The author of the stage play must therefore frequently endure the bitter consequences of these role allocations, meaning suffering the consequences of what he or she has inflicted on the partner. This could be infidelity, retreating into work, aggression, rage episodes or, in the worst of cases, illnesses and compulsive behaviors. Chain reactions result, and the merry-go-round of destiny begins to revolve.

Accordingly, the playwright is required to reckon with the partner's reactions to the role assignments and must become aware that the partnership can only remain for a limited time in this form – in fact, only for as long as the partner can tolerate the adjustment. But the inevitable breakup can be accelerated if one retaliates to the unpleasant reactions produced in the partner with responses that are themselves negative (for example, with pressure or reprimands).

Some people are lucky enough to find partners who are in fact willing to play the role in their biography. If a partner succeeds in fulfilling the expected role assignment, the role and role play are suddenly no longer sufficient because the role has now been extended and enhanced. The role assignment moves beyond the original dissatisfaction to include ever more expectations and tasks. The list of requests is constantly expanded, to the point where the partner becomes exhausted from all the attempts to provide satisfaction (trying everything) and burns out, becomes ill, or ends the relationship.

Those choosing to put up a **defense** against the role the partner is assigning face a stacked deck, since they will then no longer be loved. The reason is because the partner can only love someone who can be integrated into his or her 'world', into the biographical film, someone who can be expected to play the desired role.

There is also an unconscious negotiation frequently present in a partner relationship: if you take on the role I expect of you, then I will fulfill the role you expect of me. One of my clients expressed this directly: "If he participates in the leisure activities I have in mind for him, accompanies me to visit my friends and family, and gives me a little financial support, then I can go with him to the soccer pitch and also play the role he expects me to play in bed."

Each of the two partners, therefore, needs to make an offer that entices the other into accepting the desired role. It is necessary, as it were, to bait the hook so that the partner can bite it. Still, some people use inedible bait that is attractive to no one, or they bait it with something that is not bait at all. They believe that their offer is their bait when in fact there is nothing on the hook, or possibly even something that discourages their fish from biting.

And there is more: if this role that the partner is supposed to enact in one's biographical film were in fact played out in a puppet theater, laughter would fill the room. The only one unable to laugh about it would be the actual actor. To the contrary, he or she would probably have a hostile reaction or even leave the theater in a huff. He would mount a tremendous defense to keep from carrying out this role assignment.

Is there a solution for role allocations?

Yes, there is. It consists of three levels of development:

1. Each partner becomes aware of the role they have envisioned for the other.
2. Each becomes aware of the role they are expected to play for the other.
3. They each fulfill for themselves that which the partner is unwilling to perform, since this would otherwise place the partner in self-denial, and they jointly live out that which gives them pleasure together.

There could be a different solution, but it is one where very few couples are willing to take a chance: before embarking on the relationship, each individual writes down the role he or she expects the other to play. These 'job descriptions' are exchanged so that each participant will know precisely what to expect. Each can say to the other, "Yes, I can imagine playing this role" or "No, this role is not right for me."

In this way, the partners can avoid long detours and wrong tracks and will not find themselves many years later in the position of realizing, at the cost of a great deal of pain and suffering, that the roles they assigned to each other do not fit, or even that all the roles they expect their partner to play are only based on their own deficiencies that they themselves must overcome.

But there is also the possibility of bartering and making attainable, up-front compromises with one's partner.

The most elegant and efficient solution, however, is this: to recognize that the role allocation is a substitute for asking the partner to satisfy one's own necessities. This means distinguishing between one's own needs and substitute needs. In the case of a substitute need, it is important to ask the question: for what true need is this the substitute? Substitute needs are not genuine needs, and their satisfaction is not true fulfillment. To demand that a substitute need be satisfied is therefore a Sisyphean task for both the one demanding satisfaction as well as the one prepared to provide it.

It is important to grasp the situation: someone who has striven for years and decades to sway a partner to fulfill his or her own expectations has waged this fight for nothing and may have even terminated relationships for the wrong reasons.

But even if the partner should in fact manage to act out all assigned roles – which very seldom occurs – this does not lead to fulfillment, since one's own deficiencies, which are the cause of the role allocations, are still present. And the true needs underlying these have still not been satisfied.

If, for example, a woman needs her partner's appreciation, she forms certain expectations about the ways in which he should demonstrate this appreciation – perhaps that he presents her with flowers every week, take her to elegant restaurants, or propose to her. Her partner then finds himself in a role assignment designed to compensate for her arrested self-esteem. Another woman may suffer from the same deficiency, but her concept of appreciation involves her partner taking her on a world trip or buying her a stylish house.

No matter: even if he makes his best efforts to meet all these expectations, the man in each of these examples will never be able to compensate for the woman's low self-esteem – it would be like a filling a bottomless barrel. And even if he really succeeds in truly valuing her, the woman would not be able to do anything with this because in each case she has focused on her expectation of the form this appreciation would take.

The reason is that each person can only compensate for his or her own low self-esteem. This can occur if we become aware that it is only children who are loved and valued purely for themselves, whereas it is essential that adults develop a set of resources or skills to provide a real basis for the esteem.

It is difficult to value a partner's substitute feelings and substitute capabilities. Esteem can be bestowed, however, for such qualities as tenderness, caring, lively spirit ...

If the women in the two examples provided above bring these or other true qualities into the relationship, they no longer need to demand appreciation tied to a specific action. They can simply receive it without having to fight for it.

We are not at home where our abode is, but rather where we are understood.
CHRISTIAN MORGENSTERN

The ten unrealistic types of love

For most people, love is the most beautiful thing in the world. This feeling seems to be the only thing that could be salvaged from paradise and incorporated into the collective neurosis (see the explanation of terms in the Appendix). Unfortunately, however, love has also been subject to distortions of the collective neurosis that have far-reaching consequences for a couple's life together. It is important to be aware of these distortions so that we can understand the many conflicts and problems that affect a relationship or marriage and put them into perspective.

Simply because we constantly accept in good faith that our love for our current partner is the only true and genuine love, any crisis in the relationship or separation from that partner is bound up with enormous psychological pain. And not only that! Many physical ailments are the consequence or reflection of such psychological and mental conflicts. But in the moment when an individual sees that love is only an unconscious role play in the collective neurosis and understands the part love is playing in this process, he or she awakens to reality, understanding this situation for the first time and thus becoming largely resistant to heartache, moodiness, psychosomatic illnesses or even thoughts of suicide.

Let us summarize what has been learned from the discussion to this point by laying out the ten unrealistic types of love:

1. <u>Love based on father, mother, brother, or sister transference</u>

We have already described the phenomenon of transference in detail.

2. <u>Love of a counter-image (one's father, mother, brother or sister)</u>

If a person has not formed good relationships with his or her father, mother, or siblings, the psyche of that person forms a counter-image to them.

For example, if a mother was disorganized and not especially tidy, her son can develop a love of her counter-image – i.e., he may show love for women who are very disciplined and neat.

If a daughter had to suffer because her father did not care enough about her, it may happen that she only prefers men who provide a very high level of caring and protection.

People who have developed a counter-image to someone from an earlier relationship frequently want to coach their partner to be congruent with this counter-image. Often, they passionately do their utmost to accomplish this – a hopeless undertaking. This is because each person is his or her own individual and therefore is not simply in the world to correspond to the counter-image present in the partner's psyche.

1. Love of one's own counter-image

This is a case of totally identifying with the partner and believing that he or she is one's exact equivalent in the opposite sex. This is frequently accompanied by the notion that the partners in the relationship were predestined to be together. The realization comes eventually, however, that this dream prince or princess is merely a person like everyone else – in other words, making mistakes and revealing shortcomings that stand in contrast to one's earlier conception. In this way, the couple passes through the seven phases of identification: euphoria, recognition of reality, stagnation, frustration, reduction, resignation and, finally, apathy. While the partner is seen only through rose-colored glasses in the euphoric phase, the feeling is present by the apathetic phase that the partner is a serious head case. It needs to be considered that this is the same person! In the end, the partner is loved not for him- or herself but rather as one's own conception being projected onto the partner.

2. Love of the male or female image

In contrast to the love of one's own conception, here the love for the partner is simply for embodying femininity or masculinity per se, for being an ideal representative of the gender.

3. Love for the other's adjustment and defense mechanisms

In this type of love, one primarily loves the defense and adjustment mechanisms that the partner exhibits. These are either one's same preferred mechanisms or those needed to complement one's own personality: for example, feeling attracted to a partner who has sublimated his or her instincts or who loves the same symbols, such as garden gnomes or porcelain ducks, that serve as a substitute for true attachments; or being in awe of the partner for symbolically acting out feelings – expressing aggression by driving fast, for instance.

4. Love of co-neurosis

This is a dependent love such as the love of the helpless for the helper, of the masochist for the sadist, or of the co-dependent for the addict. This love usually only lasts for as long as the dependency relationship is maintained. Once the alcoholic has broken the addiction or the helpless individual no longer requires assistance, the relationship's great vulnerability is exposed.

5. Love of the symbol

A person can also be totally obsessed with a partner who symbolically compensates for his or her own deficiencies.

In this type of love, a specific characteristic of the person acquires such powerful significance that other qualities and idiosyncrasies take a back seat: the partner is loved merely for this symbolic compensation and for a specific feature, not for him- or herself.

6. Love for an assigned role

In this case, the love is for that partner who neatly fulfills the roles that have been assigned. Should the day come when the partner refuses to meet those role expectations, the love would be quickly extinguished.

7. Love for oneself

This is loving oneself in one's partner (narcissistic love) – seeing in the partner a great many similarities to oneself. The awe that such people find in themselves is what also fascinates them in their partner.

8. Love as an object of stabilization

Just as an alcoholic does not acknowledge being unconsciously intertwined with the addict, a person who complains about a partner being run-of-the-mill, weak, or stupid cannot understand that he or she needs precisely this partner with exactly this specific feature to stabilize his or her own personality system – for example, to feel particularly intelligent compared with a 'stupid' partner. If the partner had the same intelligence level or perhaps a higher level, this relationship would not work.

While at the conscious level one would in fact enjoy having an intelligent person as a partner, the unconscious knows that it is better to attract a less intelligent partner. Furthermore, the partner is possibly not stupid at all but has merely been so judged for the purpose of functioning as the object of stabilization.

It is important to be aware of this mechanism to be able to cease the whining and complaining. In addition, it must also become clear that separation of the partners cannot be the solution wherever the need remains for one of them to self-stabilize: supposing a breakup were to occur without resolution of the issue, the unconscious would anyway just attract another 'stupid', 'run-of-the-mill' or 'weak' partner.

In all these cases, therefore, the individual will remain an unconscious actor in a stage play who does not know the script until progress can be made toward mastering his or her true needs, assets, and qualities.

No matter how love may appear when contorted through any of its ten unrealistic types, it is still better to love and be loved based on an illusion than to experience no love at all. All these unrealistic types of love essentially represent important development steps along the way to true love. This is because it is only in realizing what is unrealistic that we can gain an awareness of what true love means.

The following statements illustrate the conviction with which such unrealistic love is expressed:

- I would love you if only you were not the way you are.
- I would love you if only you would fit my conception of you.
- I would love you if you would only fit my conception of a woman or a man.
- I would love you if you would only embody my ideal partner.
- I would love you if you would only fit my sexual fantasy.
- I would love you if only you were the way I need you to be.
- I would love you if only you fulfilled all my role allocations.
- I would love you if only you preferred the same adjustment mechanism as I do.
- I would love you if only you were the way my mother or my father were.
- I would love you if only you were the counter-image of my father or my mother.

Questions for reflection concerning mother, father, and role allocations

The following questions for reflection should provide a stimulation for us to contemplate our individual issues and our own relationship. Moreover, it would be very helpful to involve our partner in a discussion of these matters. In this way, we can succeed in advancing toward greater reality, since a sustainable relationship can only be built based on reality.

- How is it possible that the wrong person can in fact be the right person for me?
- How would I describe my physical mother?
- How can I find the true mother in me?
- What sort of relationship did I have with my physical father?
- How can I find my true father in me?
- What consequences for my destiny can be traced back to my positive or negative image of my father and mother?
- Why do role allocations occur in a partner relationship?
- Growing up, what role did I play within my family?
- Is there a role that would fit me? What is that role?
- What role did I designate for my partner?
- What role did my partner assign to me?
- How do my partner and I 'profit' from our respective role allocations?
- Will I only be loved if I play the role that my partner has assigned to me?
- Does my partner have to deny him/herself to fulfill my role expectations?
- Is it possible for us to speak openly about our role allocations and in that way break free from them?

PART THREE
Coaching to attract a compatible partner

Nothing changes until we do. Then suddenly everything changes.

Change begins with us

Most people who set out to find a partner should first schedule a coaching session – either self-coaching or coaching conducted by another person. Why? Because they will otherwise embark on the partner search accompanied by their false self-image, unconscious programs, and old beliefs. Nor does it change anything to go on many blind dates or receive matchmaking proposals on the Internet. This is because people carry the package from their past into each new encounter, resulting in blind spots, false perceptions of others, and yet another choice of the 'wrong' partner.

This condemns them to practice merely a new kind of illusive love, remaining cut off from their own development. Only once the old emotional patterns and unrealistic attitudes are changed will they stand a chance of finding a partner in real life or on the Internet who can unite with them in a successful relationship.

Coaching is thus frequently recommendable because simply becoming aware of the factors that inhibit and strain a relationship and having good intentions are still not enough to have a positive effect on one's life.

It is important for the unconscious that the individual engage in what are known as trust-building steps. Taking steps to build trust means truly implementing what we have become aware of and have relearned; adopting other ways of feeling, thinking, and acting; behaving differently; developing resources and skills; leaving behind the old ways and setting aside the errors we are seemingly condemned to repeat; taking actions that lead away from the old influences and the old stage play into a place where free choice is possible.

The old programs can only be deleted when new ones are experienced! The unconscious can no longer perpetuate the previous attraction of persons and events, instead staging enjoyable partner situations and fateful events based on the newly developed, realistic beliefs and other behaviors. Just as a trainer can induce an athlete to attain maximum performance, a coach has the role of assisting clients to maximize their lives in accordance with their own identity.

Coaching is sometimes so remarkably simple that the question is frequently raised why clients have not found the solution on their own long before now. When someone appears in our 'film', however, it is not at all easy to stop and view the scene from a birds-eye perspective. A coach, on the other hand, can detect the essentials in a client's life history, and frequently the greatest changes can be brought about by small details.

A good yet brief example is the case of Gerald, who works as a web designer. Although he was 34 years old, Gerald had never experienced sex with a woman. Wishing finally to change this situation, he turned to coaching.

Gerald grew up without a father and thus had little opportunity to encounter a masculine role model. At his first coaching session, the following success-limiting behaviors became evident:

1. Upon becoming acquainted with a woman, Gerald would bombard her with texts, emails, and phone calls without giving her the opportunity to respond to these. In this way, he revealed his neediness. Feeling pressured, women cut off their contact with him after a short time.
2. He would pour out his heart to them on their first date, openly exhibiting his feelings and his psychological pain.
3. He would tell women on the first date that he had never been intimate with a woman.
4. He owns two automobiles: an upper-middle-class sedan and a classic car that he dearly loves, keeping the replacement parts for it in his home. He routinely drove the classic car on dates, believing that the woman would share his enthusiasm for old cars.
5. He lives in a loft on the upper floor of a town house, sharing the staircase with the owners.
6. He is not involved in athletic pursuits, and riding his bicycle to work is his only physical activity.
7. He is uneasy when speaking.

His coach proposed the following steps:

1. He should make a rule only to send carefully written texts, and only after receiving a response. He should avoid compet-

ing with women in the sharing of feelings – in other words, not disclose his private sentiments on the first date.

2. He needs to keep to himself the fact that has not yet slept with a woman.
3. A large part of his sexual energy is tied up in his classic car. To free up this energy, he was encouraged to move the car lower on his priority list, storing the spare parts in the garage to enhance his appeal to visitors to his home.
4. It was recommended that he move out of the loft in the town house, which created too great an involvement with the owner's family (unconscious parental transfer). Every visit by a woman to the loft could be observed by the owners of the town house. These 'substitute parents' would certainly ask themselves: Is he alone? If not, who else is there with him? Has this woman been there before? Is she right for him? Will she spend the night?
5. In short: He needs to live where he can act freely and not be under constant observation.
6. The athletic activities most suited to giving his masculinity a boost are contests against one or more opponents. Aggressiveness and competition are associated with increased testosterone release. The higher testosterone level will cause the opposite sex to perceive him as manlier and more athletic.
7. To increase his speaking confidence, he was assigned to enroll in communication training.

Soon after Gerald had made the first revisions to his behaviors and thoughts, he noticed that something in his life had changed for the better and that the people around him were friendlier and more sympathetic to him. The changes also motivated him to approach the next tasks with enthusiasm.

By the end of six months, Gerald had completed all seven steps that had been agreed upon in his coaching sessions. He was unrecognizable. He had become a real man. After four months, he met Sarah, with whom he was emotionally and spiritually compatible and with whom he also achieved sexual satisfaction. Today Gerald cannot understand what took him so long to develop a functioning partner relationship.

Recognize 'life inhibitors' and free yourself from them

A somewhat different situation is presented in the case of Andrea: Andrea is the daughter of a couple who belonged to a religious cult. The many religious rituals and rigid restrictions in nearly all areas of life drove her to leave home at age 16. She eventually encountered Carla, a 47-year-old woman, and moved into her apartment. The two of them jointly signed the apartment lease and opened a shared bank account. Andrea was elated to have found a real home with Carla.

After some time, however, Carla revealed herself as a new life inhibitor. She increasingly slipped into the role of a controller and detective. She monitored Andrea's mobile phone, read her emails, and forbade her to go out with young men.

Twelve years later, Carla reached the moment when she could no longer keep Andrea from growing up, and she arranged a husband for Andrea. John was a shy and self-conscious man who remained Andrea's partner for ten years although she could not love him. Feeling increasingly unhappy, Andrea decided to seek out coaching as a means of finally achieving a vibrant and fulfilling relationship.

Based on Andrea's previous history and her present unfortunate situation, it was clear that her vital energies were bound up in her relationship with Carla, their commonly held lease and bank account, and her partner relationship with John. These commitments inevitably resulted in the following steps:

Andrea was encouraged to end the relationship with Carla, who had played the role of mother substitute for Andrea. In addition, it was important for her to terminate the shared lease agreement and close the joint bank account. She also needed to find her own living situation if she hoped to achieve an independent life. Finally, separation from John was advisable, since the development of both partners would otherwise remain blocked.

After Andrea had completed these five steps, she could gradually start to stand on her own feet. Before long, she met Frank, with whom she entered an intimate, loving relationship. Andrea was amazed when, after 22 years, her parents suddenly contacted her. Andrea was able to build a good relationship with her parents without becoming subservient to them.

The cases of Gerald and Andrea underline how important it is to free bound-up and misdirected energies. The list below illustrates where energies can be bound up:

- In roles (buddy, helper, spoiled child, etc.)
- In compulsive behaviors
- In conscious and unconscious projections
- In unconscious father, mother, brother, or sister transference
- In an over-dimensioned relationship to one's child (substitute partner, child as substitute for the child in oneself in relationship to one's father or mother)
- In over-dimensioned love for a house pet (only where the pet acts as substitute child or partner)
- In fixations (on a guru, for example)
- In an illness (energy somatization)
- In material objects (classic car, stamp collection, etc.)
- In identifications (clubs, ideologies, etc.)
- In sublimations
- In symbols
- In sexual perversion

Self-coaching

Everything we do in our psyche or inner life also has its virtual reflection in our outer experiences. This includes the law of attraction, the law of psychological kinship, and the 'internal equals external' law (these and other laws are explained in the Appendix).

Specifically, this means that everyone who suppresses an inner need creates situations in the outer world in which this need is similarly not accepted. If one lies to oneself, for example, this will result in being lied to by others. Or if someone constantly engages in self-criticism, that person will also be criticized in the external world.

But the corresponding opposite to an inner feeling can also be engaged: those who harbor feelings of guilt in their psyche will be punished by others under the old-fashioned guilt-atonement principle. The guilty feeling is thus balanced by atonement, its opposite.

In that sense, what is crucial to one's own destiny is how it appears on the inside, **what one does with oneself**. At heart, very few people understand what they do with themselves or how they treat themselves because they are usually so totally trapped in old feelings, ways of thinking, patterns, and programs that they cannot develop sufficient distance to gain a clear perspective on their own inner lives.

The individual believes that external circumstances are immovable and unchangeable. In fact, however, the external world and how an individual comes to experience it are to a large extent only a reflection of the individual's internal world or its opposite. For those who wish to achieve a better life, therefore, it is eminently important to gain insight about themselves and to recognize:

- how they deceive themselves
- how they outsmart themselves
- how they fight with themselves
- how they devalue themselves
- how they lie to themselves
- how they block themselves
- how they contradict themselves
- how they sabotage themselves
- how they play a role for themselves
- how they keep up appearances for themselves
- how they play games with themselves and others
- how they punish themselves
- how (and why) they follow rules or dictate them to others
- how they reward themselves
- how they compensate for their shortcomings in one area of life with another area of life
- how they avoid awareness
- how they use repression
- how they run away from problems and conflicts
- how they avoid responsibility
- how they shun reality

This self-reflection enables us to recognize our own internal world and in so doing to develop a greater understanding of its external setting. The goal is to proceed from changing our inner world – i.e., setting aside old emotional patterns and outdated beliefs – to achieving a change in the situations and conditions of the outer world. Constantly wanting to battle or change only the external symptoms is a senseless, futile endeavor. Until we die, of course, there is good that can be done. While the ceiling will never fall in on us out of boredom, it is also true that this is no way to achieve an especially joyful life. The best thing is gradually to put an end to the inner maneuvering and to create our own new conditions in the external world through new, reality-based ways of feeling and thinking. What remains will be merely a small 'residual destiny risk' we can live with.

Learn from the sun to give warmth
Learn from the moon to change
Learn from the stars to be one of many
Learn from the earth to be motherly
Learn from the clouds to float
Learn from the wind to provide impulse
Learn from the storm to be powerful
Learn from the rain to penetrate
Learn from the trees to stand tall
Learn from the leaves to let go
Learn from the flowers to blossom
Learn from the plants of spring to renew
Learn from the stones to remain
Learn from the birds to soar
Learn from the seasons that life always begins again
INDIAN PROVERB

Bound-up energies as the cause of attraction to the wrong partner and difficulties in relationships

Susan (41) suffers greatly from being single for the last several years. To be sure, potential partners appeared in her life from time to time, but they were unwilling to commit to her. These men were either already married or looking for a brief affair, or they greatly valued their freedom and only occasionally contacted her. Susan's most ardent wish, however, is to be in a permanent relationship.

Her conversations clarify the situation: she consciously wishes for a relationship while unconsciously she does everything to prevent one from developing. This discrepancy between her conscious and unconscious desires creates a difficulty that influences both partner attraction as well as the course of a partner relationship.

But how is it possible for Susan unconsciously to repel what she so intensely desires? Susan's energies are already bound up in her extremely strong commitment to her job, in an over-dimensioned relationship to her daughter Michelle (17), and in her alcohol addiction (she drinks a bottle of wine every night).

These three bonds leave no room in her life for a partner, and, viewed realistically, she would also have no energy and no time for an additional commitment. Since she is still not aware of this fact, however, she believes that she has the capacity to form a relationship while her potential partners are unable to connect or bond.

It is a widespread phenomenon that people cannot see their own blocking and resistance maneuvers since they do not recognize these as affecting their own relationship-forming capacity.

Basically, the very individual who absolutely wishes to form a relationship and so dearly hopes to develop closeness to a partner unconsciously creates distance. Such distance-creating maneuvers discourage a potential partner from drawing closer. After all, why should a person be interested in increased closeness and bonding when in fact no space for him or her exists there?

It is even worse than this: from the outset, our unconscious resistance efforts attract the 'wrong' partners: the ones with whom it is impossible to bond because they have some sort of defect or handicap. And the 'wrong' partners experience the same thing.

We could go as far as to say: someone who unconsciously avoids relationships ...

- ☐ allows distance to develop
- ☐ allows confusion in the relationship

- ☐ allows affairs
- ☐ allows separation to take place
- ☐ allows divorce to be filed for

The unconscious avoider of relationships uses the conscious avoider of relationships for these actions, thus producing a situation where the conscious avoider will suffer.

	Attraction	
unconsciously	↔	consciously
creates		creates distance
distance		(opposite pole perverted through repression)

Very similar to the situation of the unconscious and conscious avoider of relationships is that involving unconscious and conscious selfishness. It frequently happens in our seminars that women complain of always attracting selfish men. There are causes here as well that usually escape conscious perception.

If a woman always pursues only her subjective tastes, refusing to portray herself as 'friendly to men', exclusively living out her own lifestyle and seeking to impose her own views, the man receives nothing useful from her, nothing that satisfies his needs.

This represents unconscious selfishness on the part of the woman that results in conscious selfishness on the part of the man. He is unwilling to give her anything, is close-fisted with his finances, and is also starting to be stingy with his time as well. In other words, he is distancing himself. The woman's unconscious selfishness, namely being parsimonious with her charm, only achieving her own ambitions, and not providing the man with what he would need to feel loved by her, is complementarily related to the man's conscious selfishness.

She then complains that she only meets self-indulgent men or those who are inclined to be tight with money, without realizing that she herself awakens these qualities in her partners. She whines about the situations she causes, wishes to confront these indications, or hopes that one day a generous man will appear who loves her the way she is.

Based on the laws described above, however, her wish will never be fulfilled unless she becomes aware of her unconscious selfishness, unless she herself becomes more generous and sensitive, until she satisfies some of her partner's needs. Then the picture can change, and the problem will disappear.

Most of the great evils that man has inflicted on man have come through people feeling quite certain about something which, in fact, was false.
BERTRAND RUSSELL

Changing one's beliefs

For most people, it is only after a personal tragedy that they are ready to rethink and alter their beliefs. Unless they are reduced to living in total squalor, they hold onto their beliefs like a shipwreck survivor clinging to a plank.

It is impossible to help them, and they do not welcome assistance since they seek to proselytize others with their false beliefs. And yet others, were they to become converted to these beliefs, would likely experience the same illnesses and personal tragedies as the 'missionaries' themselves. Additionally, the beliefs of these proselytizers are a form of compensation for their deficiencies. They cannot let go of these, lest they become unbalanced or even find themselves left with nothing at all, or because they fear that the worst thing (unconsciously) imaginable would happen: they would be forced to develop their resources and capacities and thus fill in their deficiencies.

For it takes a great deal of courage to own up to one's own shortcomings, even privately.

Beliefs can develop in many ways. Usually they can be traced back to parents and grandparents, individual influences, script-specific experiences (reinforcement of beliefs), deficiencies, cultural traditions, social conventions, morals, common practices, customs, tradition, cultural milieu, authority figures, historical period, one's friendship circles, school, and university. One single false doctrine can be sufficient to affect one's own life adversely. Examples of such false doctrines include the following: "I am waiting for Prince Charming" or "I don't give a damn about money" or "I will always live an ascetic life".

Most of these doctrines generate many spinoffs. These new doctrines produce additional adverse effects on a person's destiny. Besides causing him or her to be attracted to the 'wrong' individuals and events, such doctrines also constantly result in other people being secretly or openly devalued, with inevitable damage to interpersonal relations.

Standards and beliefs regarding what counts as good and bad are also widespread: people are attacked or rejected for being bad from one's own perspective. Such standards include the following:

- Rivalry is bad
- Wealth is bad
- Possessions are bad
- Status and prestige are bad
- Boundaries are bad
- Pleasure is bad
- The ego is bad
- The intellect is bad
- Sex is bad
- Flexibility is bad
- Criticism is bad
- Striving for power is bad
- Ambition is bad
- Hierarchy is bad
- Unmasking and revealing standards of good and bad is bad

It is easy to imagine the extent to which a relationship can suffer if one partner is 'bad', even if that partner's 'wrongdoing' only checks off two or three of the items on the above list. In such a case, almost every day is filled with nothing but anger and conflict, since the way that partner is, is wrong!

Thus, we see how a negative doctrine attacks, represses, restricts, blocks, confuses, weakens, unsettles, disintegrates, creates contradictions.

Below are a few ways in which doctrines can affect a cult member, for example:

- They constrict
- They make a taboo out of entire areas of life (like pleasure, sexuality, freedom)
- They limit information
- They affect encounters (other people recoil, offer no advice, etc.)
- They restrict partner choice
- They have a negative effect on careers
- They cause physical ailments because important life energies are not permitted to be experienced

Looking more closely at doctrines and beliefs, these constitute laws that govern the individual. Put another way: unconscious beliefs take on the character of laws: in life they function as laws of destiny and thus appear as a higher spiritual power that rules over us: when, like puppets, we perform the programs of our inherited beliefs and their related role assignments, our similarly connected destiny is bestowed upon us.

Frequently a discrepancy exists between conscious and unconscious beliefs. Such a difference exists if a person consciously believes: "I would like to get rich and live in material comfort" but unconsciously harbors the belief that "I would rather stay poor because it is noble and good to be poor."

In this respect, it is evident that what is a person consciously declares does not equate to what that person's unconscious feels and thinks. And it is also clear that we should not take so seriously what people say.

When the individual brings unconscious beliefs into conscious awareness, this action creates an opportunity to make corrections and chart a new course. It is important to reflect on the beliefs listed below: beliefs about ...

- ☐ one's own ego
- ☐ money
- ☐ family
- ☐ raising children
- ☐ work
- ☐ medicine (conventional, natural, etc.)
- ☐ one's own attractiveness
- ☐ one's own image as a man
- ☐ one's own image as a woman
- ☐ the partner relationship
- ☐ world view
- ☐ philosophy of life
- ☐ one's own path
- ☐ God
- ☐ sexuality
- ☐ one's own calling

Beliefs of a girl who wants to be a boy

Susan's parents were expecting a boy. At an early age, this situation caused her to develop the reactive attitude that "I want to be better than any man." Later, as an adult woman, she became extremely frustrated at repeatedly seeing that the only men who showed interest in her were those she considered to be weak. In addition, things were not going well for her sexually.

In her coaching sessions, Susan declared, "I really want a man who is superior to me and whom I can be proud of. I would like to find a man with style and class and not always have to deal with weak, worthless men. Not only that: I want to spend passionate nights with this high-caliber man. Since I have my own successful career, I would like a man who is a notch above me. And I am tired of always having to stand up for myself. This often overstresses me."

Susan's coach assigned her the task of writing down all her beliefs about men and sexuality. For Susan, men are:

- paper tigers
- weaklings
- boring
- quiet
- unromantic
- uninteresting
- greedy
- emotionally impaired
- insensitive
- uncontrolled
- hurtful
- incapable of discussion
- unable to show their emotions
- only interested in sex
- humorless
- incapable of differentiation
- cautious
- unteachable
- carnivores
- stubborn
- untrustworthy
- unreliable
- simpletons
- unimaginative
- all the same

Susan's beliefs about sexuality follow below: Sex ...

- ☐ is complicated
- ☐ is boring
- ☐ is damaging
- ☐ is uncomfortable
- ☐ is not beautiful
- ☐ hurts
- ☐ is distasteful
- ☐ is awkward
- ☐ is obligatory
- ☐ is binding
- ☐ you have to do it
- ☐ is immoral
- ☐ is degrading
- ☐ is undignified
- ☐ is unsanitary
- ☐ means subjection
- ☐ why?
- ☐ is disgusting
- ☐ is annoying
- ☐ means accommodation
- ☐ means close your eyes and get through it

Her beliefs concerning men revealed her need for weak men based on the way she was raised. She needs to be able to compete with them and defeat them.

She unconsciously chooses weak men or, through the lens of her upbringing, looks for men's weaknesses and blocks out their strengths to feel herself superior to them. Moreover, her own criteria form the sole basis for judging whether a man is strong or weak. At bottom, only she can be her ideal man.

There is still another point that needs to be kept in mind: there is always a connection between that which we judge and experience through our own masculinity or femininity and the viewpoint of the opposite sex. Just as a man who has problems expressing his masculinity develops a false image of women, Susan's psyche – until she completely affirms her femininity – will harbor a false image of men that always strives to be affirmed and reinforced through external experiences.

It is possible to diagram Anya's dilemma as follows:

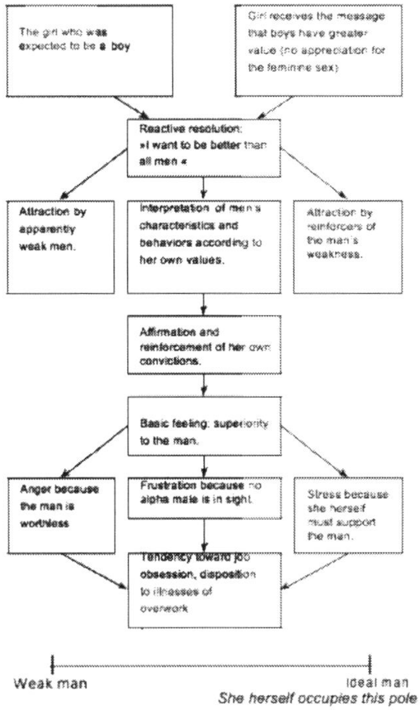

At this point, Susan must ask the question: Do I want to relive my previous destiny – namely, my disappointment in only attracting weaklings even though I seek a first-rate man, added to the anger, displeasure, frustration, and stress I experience with weak men – or do I want to form a better partner relationship by changing my attitude?

Here too, we see in Susan the widespread discrepancy between conscious and unconscious beliefs. In her conscious, she wants a strong man, and yet her unconscious has a completely different opinion: based on her upbringing, her unconscious attracts only weak men or men whom she can judge to be weak using her own standards of interpretation.

In this connection, it is also important to distinguish three types of experience:

1. <u>Experience based on one's influences</u>

This is subjective experience that is not objectively sustainable. For example: her subjective experiences with men does not entitle Susan to make a blanket statement that "men today are all weak!"

2. <u>Experience based on repetition</u>

Even if adverse events continue to repeat themselves, this still does not mean that these constitute valid experience. For example: it is possible to act inappropriately or perform an activity incorrectly for 30 years. Thus, Susan would be able to recount her fictive competitions with men over many years.

3. Valid experience

Such an experience is objectively justifiable and corresponds to reality. Susan would recognize that there are both weak and strong men, insensitive men and less sensitive ones, good lovers and those not so good ...

In this case, she would have abandoned her script and her film and would awaken to reality.

To succeed in life, you need two things: ignorance and confidence.
MARK TWAIN

Illusive and realistic positive self-image

Many people think of themselves as strong in areas where they are in fact incapable and week. Nadja, for example, believes herself to be a good driver. The truth is that she lacks concentration, commits many driving errors, fails to drive proactively, and is the cause of two or three accidents nearly every year.

Hubert, on the other hand, believes that he is well-informed. In fact, he gets his information entirely from the tabloid press.

Here, a positive belief that a person is expert in a specific area does not automatically mean that the belief is indeed true. On the contrary, the positive belief keeps the person from avoiding mistakes, making progress, and achieving improvement in that area. An even less auspicious example would be the case of people who claim that they are unafraid. This is because such people have succeeded in converting their subjective opinion into an apparently objective law by maintaining, “If you are afraid of something, that is what you will attract.” The phrase is then parroted by millions, while a fearful individual may be labeled as pathological and directed into therapy.

The reality looks quite different, however: fearful people (except those with anxiety neurosis), based on their information or their intellectual complexity, have an ability to recognize dangers others do not see, and they can defend themselves against these: their fear functions as a life preserver. Fearless individuals, on the other hand, have merely repressed their fears – and only repressed fears invite calamity, in accordance with the law of the return of the repressed (see appendix).

An example of an illusive positive self-image is Brent (36). He aspires to rise in his profession and find a partner with whom a beautiful relationship is possible. His career requires him to deal intensively with specialized written matter and attend management and executive seminars. To be happy in a partner relationship, he would have to adjust physically, mentally, and emotionally to his partner, learn to be more attentive, and become a better lover – creating a conflict with his earlier rough and egoistical behavior.

Brent, hearing this, cries out: "But I want to remain who I am! I do not want to have to change!"

Such an adjustment and consequence only constitute the right approach, however, in cases where group influence and pressure predominate or where one is required to bend to another person's will or expectation – but not where individual improvement is required, where there is an opportunity to develop true skills, to grow and, in so doing, to please oneself and others.

Put another way: if the ego to which one wants to remain loyal lacks substance or even shows destructive tendencies, then it is not advantageous (in the sense of a happy future) to remain "who I am."

Nevertheless, a great many people spend their lives being the guard dog that protects their illusive (thoroughly positive) self-image. They are continually occupied with hiding their incapability from themselves and others and never revealing it. They suffer from what is called a 'God complex' and already believe themselves to be perfect and infallible: they do not need to develop themselves further – only the others must change.

The message they send out says, "Don't just point out my inadequacies, weaknesses and deficiencies, because you can get to know me from a different side!" For this reason, the strong individuals are not those who constantly gloss over their weaknesses but those who have the courage to recognize their lack of ability and turn this into capability. To admit one's incapacity and weaknesses and, in the end, transform them into strengths is one of the greatest accomplishments that anyone can achieve. Only denied incapacities and weaknesses lead to psychological pain and misfortune.

For example: one whose abilities with respect to partner relationships reveal many shortcomings and weaknesses will witness the failure of all such relationships as life progresses and will therefore be forced to endure psychological pain and possibly even illness. Based on these deficiencies, it is often even possible to predict these unsuccessful relationships, since clearly such a person's individual 'offer' can and will bring no happiness to any partner, let alone to him- or herself. This is because each demonstration of incapability is an unconscious attack on the partner, a lack of respect for the partner. Feeling the lack of something, the partner reacts negatively and, as a result, precipitates pain and illness once again.

Governed by an illusive positive self-image, an individual can only perceive the partner's attack, while his or her own aggressive provocation of the partner remains unseen.

So: what is the difference between an illusive positive self-image and a realistic positive self-image? In the former case, shortcomings and weaknesses are whitewashed when the person acts as if he or she is all-knowing and in full possession of all resources and capabilities. The illusive positive self-image is like a soap bubble: at any moment it can burst and vanish.

A realistic positive self-image is present when a person, knowing that all human nature with all its resources and capabilities lies within him or her, has confidence that all these traits can be learned and set in motion if the determination to do so exists. The person understands the potential of these resources but is also aware of still possessing weaknesses and deficiencies, recognizing the areas where there remains a need to diversify, improve and develop capabilities. He or she contemplates the future realistically and optimistically, and this optimism, in contrast to that of someone with an illusive positive self-image, is justified. Such a person can seize the future, make corrections or changes, and proceed strategically.

Questions for reflection concerning beliefs

- Where do I continually evade reality?
- Are there situations where I continually punish myself?
- Where do I deceive myself about things?
- Am I one of the unconscious or conscious relationship avoiders?
- Am I truly ready for a relationship?
- What doctrines do I have concerning a partner relationship?
- What are my doctrines regarding the opposite sex?
- What doctrines do I have concerning family?
- What effect do my doctrines have on my surroundings and my life?
- Which doctrines can be traced to deficiencies in my personality system?
- How can I convert my weaknesses into strengths?
- How can I become aware of my unconscious doctrines?
- How can I change my doctrines if they do not correspond to reality?

PART FOUR
The conscious couple

In principle, every person's nature has the capacity to achieve a high degree of wisdom. Previous cultures have, however, permitted such attainment only in exceptional cases. As a whole, humanity exhibits no wisdom. It resembles a bacterial strain that propagates as long as its basic needs are met. Culture thus needs renewal: a humanistic orientation!
MARIE VON EBNER-ESCHENBACH

First and second nature

All of us have two natures within us: our first nature, which contains our true resources and human needs, and our second nature, which is the result of education, culture, and the influence of the time in which we live. This second nature is a consequence of the adaptive and defense mechanisms discovered by Freud, which include sublimation, imitation, regression, symbolic acting out, identification, projection, rationalization, repression, somatization, and reaction formation.

This second nature can also bring great pleasure and can balance one's own personality system – think only of art and music (sublimation), a beautiful boat or glider (symbolic acting out), interesting, exciting sporting events (identification), membership in an institution or company (identification), a pet one becomes fond of (projection), the world of the rich and beautiful that brightens the life of the average citizen (projection).

An individual's situation only becomes difficult if he or she can no longer maintain a balance in this second nature and thus must make use of other defense and adaptation mechanisms such as repression and somatization.

Or if the individual becomes so caught up in this second nature that actual capabilities and needs are overlaid with substitute capabilities and needs. How can something like this occur? When there is no access to one's own human nature and feelings and no search for one's own identity has taken place, the unconscious develops something creatively – a state of depression, for example.

In this sense, the depression is a substitute capability used by the individual to acquire a substitute identity. Others then become aware: "There goes Myriam, the one with depression." Furthermore, she can use her depression to set the overall mood around her, or can blackmail others with it. With that, she then does not need to go to work. Such cases are described as morbid gain.

Another example: a man always employs something to attract attention (this is the intention of his unconscious). He causes trouble, frequently does the opposite of what is indicated in each situation, or acts recklessly. These negative behaviors are a substitute for being able to develop originality, add variety to his life, make changes, implement new ideas, or possibly even invent something by thinking out of the box.

Going into hysterics or developing a penchant for dramatization are other examples of a substitute capability created by the unconscious to channel available energy. Drama and hysteria are orchestrated as a substitute due to a lack of capacity for sexual experience or autonomous action or an inability to excel through managing one's own life, achieving self-realization, or carrying out projects. Hysterical behavior allows a person to take center stage and 'shine' effortlessly without developing his or her own resources.

These three examples represent a wealth of substitute capabilities that are formed when their corresponding systems cannot be truly developed. Because these substitutes are so often in evidence, they have practically achieved normal status. A person cannot be blamed for these since, without psychological knowledge, it is impossible to recognize what should have been cultivated in place of them. Moreover, no one has offered encouragement to do this. Many substitute capabilities, furthermore, are inherited through our family, and it would never occur to us that some completely different response might be possible.

This plainly shows why a truly functional partner relationship is so uncommon: it is only once partners discuss all these connections between themselves and each makes the attempt to convert these substitute capabilities into actual, useful capabilities that relationships become happier and more fulfilling. If this willingness is absent, the following picture emerges: each partner experiences the feeling of being in the right, of being a good person, refusing to believe that his or her own substitute capabilities are the cause of the situation.

When needs or feelings are incompatible with one's own superego, old beliefs, or societal trends, they are *a priori* driven into the unconscious, where they can no longer be perceived and observed, let alone displayed.

Based on this situation, many people remain unaware of their true needs and are unconsciously blocked from meeting those needs.

They do not know, or know only vaguely, about their need to engage in physical exercise, to win; their need for their own turf, for safety, for communication; the need to represent themselves, to have free range of action, to create something, to show their feelings, to express their own tastes; their need for acquaintances and a partner relationship, for autonomy and their own path, for sexuality and passion, for finding their own sense of purpose, for receiving recognition, for freedom and independence for their need to live differently and find alternatives to traditional ways.

We frequently do not recognize our own needs, conflicts, and stresses. But even when these are known, we often believe that these do not matter a great deal, because the psychological pain has been banished from our consciousness into the unconscious. As a result, this pain is then symbolically expressed on the body. In other words: we do not place a high priority on the existing conflict – we have somehow resigned ourselves to the situation (state of resignation).

What so many people cannot believe if they have not dealt with the unconscious is the following:

All needs are present in every individual, but in different manifestations.

And it frequently happens that those who are especially vehement in denying the existence of a need often unconsciously long to satisfy that need.

Coaching sessions assist many people in seeing how ravenously and addictively they crave embraces, tenderness, and the spiritual aspect of love and warmth and yet fail to acknowledge these needs in either themselves or others. They simply cannot and will not believe. When this happens, the desire for tenderness reappears in other forms, whether in a sugar craving or a longing for recognition, fame, and honor. In such a case, the individual unconsciously believes that only through achieving fame and honor will it be possible to gain an abundance of attention and tenderness. And yet the present situation, devoid of recognition and honor

– at least in the individual's unconscious belief – leaves the person feeling unlovable, uninteresting, and unimportant. He or she cannot imagine the possibility of being accepted and loved by others.

People in such a situation usually did not experience unconditional love from their mother (mother love in its true sense) – i.e., they were only loved when they fulfilled their mother's expectations and role assignments, but not for the sake of themselves and their uniqueness. In this sense, they continue to believe as adults that they will only be loved based on achievement and success. Furthermore, due to a pervasive archetype, many men believe it is necessary for them to be "cool" and invulnerable if they are not to be considered unmanly. In this way, their inner child is often entirely repressed.

Particularly prone to suppressing their personal needs are individuals who are unaware of the bipolarity of all systems and energies and who therefore identify with only one of these poles. Those who identify with the decisiveness pole cannot conceive that they also carry within them the opposite pole and the desire to reveal it. Such people are unaware of their own need, usually resisting even the notion of harboring such a need.

It is even worse when needs not only go unperceived but also conflict with one another. In this way, the need for security stands at odds with the need for variety and change: the individual opting for security must necessarily suppress the need for change, and vice versa.

It also happens that the need to meet people and form a partner relationship can conflict with the need for withdrawal, quiet, and solitude. The same conditions apply here: when one need is satisfied, the other is shortchanged. A need that goes unfulfilled over time will eventually be expressed physically through the adaptive mechanism of somatization. The respective organ or organic system then symbolizes the unsatisfied need. For example, afflictions of the mucous membrane or stomach problems can represent a lack of security. Kidney and bladder problems stand for an imbalance of give-and-take between partners or a disparity related to love and erotic attraction in the partner relationship (indicating that love is rarely reciprocated).

In sum, it can be said that there are some people who are aware of their urgent need for independence and others who do not know this because curtailment of their freedom as they were growing up in their home, environment, and culture was regarded as 'normal.' For some, difficulty in appreciating their own thirst to be free results in an inability to satisfy a need for fluids. And, in comparison, how much more difficult must it be for them to perceive and admit their need for boundaries, freedom, and independence?

Here the transformation of the old morality into laws for life can help bring needs into awareness. Those who live by the saying "That which serves one's life is good, that which runs counter to it is bad" will have an easier time of it.

It is a matter of developing an increasingly keen sense of the needs present in one's personality system and how these needs can be satisfied: a sense of what is what is needed to maintain homeostasis, of what is required to come back into equilibrium and maintain that state. The admonition to "take care of yourself" is a call to do precisely that.

Become significant, my friend!
ANGELUS SILESIUS

The significance of needs gratification for the successful couple relationship

A list containing 144 human needs is found in the appendix to this book.

You should make two copies of this list and fill it out together with your partner. You will then have the basis of an enormously important discussion of your partner relationship. This conversation is necessary, since you could otherwise spend years and decades in a partner relationship without being able to achieve what you really need. The partner cannot simply guess everything that you need in all areas of your life. If you proceed in this way, it will not be necessary for you to develop ingenious role allocations to achieve your goals. Neither will you need to put up with all the negative consequences that typically accompany these role assignments. In short, you will have to contend less with miserable karma. And something else as well: because you will have absolutely no need to select your partner in advance based on your unconscious role allocation, your choice will no longer be so limited. In this process, you will see what different priorities exist and where harmony reigns. Where is it crucial for you to make sure that a need is met, and where can you ask your partner – or other individuals you know – to satisfy that need?

What strategies have you employed to this point to satiate a specific need?

Were these strategies successful, or is it time to draw up new ones?

Perhaps you can also learn from other people who generally reach their goals quickly, using their approach as a model to be modified according to your own individuality.

It should also be considered that many people unconsciously seek out environments where certain needs cannot be met, or they have unconscious defensive attitudes and old belief structures that prevent them from satisfying a need. It constantly happens that such individuals find excuses to explain why meeting some need is impossible in their own specific case.

And there remains the question of whether one's partner will permit fulfillment of these needs.

Matthew (34) has a deeply ingrained need for exercise. He places great emphasis on letting off steam three times a week by playing squash. This does not sit well with his wife Lauren (34), who would rather have him assist her with the house or yard. As a result, she constantly finds fault with him, and Matthew almost always heads for the squash court with a guilty conscience.

How could this problem be resolved? Almost every problem can be overcome in the presence of a willingness to discuss the matter and achieve mutual good will and understanding. A solution is even possible where – as in the case of Matthew and Lauren – one partner's need runs counter to the other's.

For example, Matthew could compromise with Lauren by considering where he could meet some of her critical needs or how he might support her efforts to achieve her own equilibrium. Or – if she is fixated on the house and lawn tasks – he could hire domestic hourly help if he himself has no time for this.

It is of great import in this connection that each partner understands the relevance of needs satisfaction in restoring balance to the personality system and that each is willing to act as supporter and promoter in this area. This will have a payoff, at any rate, since there will now be a more contented and balanced partner at home. Someone who is supported in achieving balance will have a better emotional state, will be in a better mood and, in addition, will rarely be sick: the quality of life for both partners and the quality of the partner relationship itself will be significantly enhanced.

People do not understand how that which is at variance with itself agrees with itself.
HERACLITUS

The solution: there are two poles to everything

The world is laid out in bipolar fashion. This fact holds momentous significance for every partner relationship, since each human being also contains two opposite poles. They are mutually related, of course, but this reciprocal 'complementarity' rarely triggers bursts of enthusiasm. A person identifies with one pole and unconsciously projects the opposite pole onto others. In this way, the unconscious contributes to keeping everything balanced. The question is only in what manner this is accomplished.

While there is usually no conscious approval of this sort of balance, the unconscious does not question it at all. Its actions simulate the way the autonomous nervous system acts on the physical level, performing its task stoically by attracting the opposite pole it needs for psychological homeostasis (the law of balance stimulates the law of attraction).

The farther removed one is from the physiological midpoint between the poles, the stronger the reaction will be, comparable to the movement of a pendulum, which swings uniformly in one direction as well as the other. Since everyone always accommodates both poles within him- or herself, this means, for example, that the oppressed is alive within the oppressor and vice versa. It is rarely advantageous, therefore, when the formerly oppressed attains a position of power, since such a person often then proves to be more rigorous and severe than the authority being displaced.

In this constant interplay, nature pursues a developmental goal between the oppressor and the oppressed as well as between the powerful and the powerless. In the end, this occurs because someone who has greatly suffered and squandered so much valuable time in power games ultimately develops own's ideas, concepts, life program, spiritual possessions, and life journey, in this way acquiring power over self.

Considered from the perspective of bipolarity, by the way, it is useless for dominant individuals to rescind their claim to power and their obsessive behavior. Because of the mutual complexity between the oppressor and the oppressed in the unconscious, the problem is not resolved in this manner since, once the oppressor no longer oppresses, the oppressed unconsciously looks for another oppressor.

Examples of the two poles that exist for every individual

egoistic	----------	altruistic
well behaved	----------	rude
weak on implementa-tion	----------	aggressive
poverty	----------	wealth
low intrinsic value	----------	excessive intrinsic value
underestimated	----------	overestimated
cast out	----------	established
tongue-tied	----------	talks to death
insecure	----------	secure
lack of creativity	----------	creativeness
illness	----------	health
unclean	----------	clean (perfect)
lazy	----------	industrious
lack of eroticism	----------	sexual fantasies
disharmony	----------	harmony
peace	----------	war
powerlessness	----------	power
repression	----------	fixation, model, guru
lack	----------	abundance
uneducated	----------	educated
vulgar	----------	noble
negative thinking	----------	positive thinking
unimportant	----------	important
bum	----------	careerist
inhibition	----------	ideal (perfection)
unfaithful	----------	faithful

joking	----------	serious
guilty	----------	innocent
slow	----------	fast
friend	----------	enemy
conforming	----------	rebellious
low demand	----------	high demand
weakness	----------	strength
lies	----------	is lied to
helpless	----------	helper

Each pole has advantages and disadvantages. For example, closeness contains the advantages of security and love. Distance has the advantages of freedom and adventure. For this reason, identification with one pole is also a question of need. Which need is stronger in me and where am I needier? I will feel myself drawn to that pole and will act out that pole.

Every identification with a pole is very strongly determined, however, by the basic need for recognition. Many people simply identify with the pole that provides them with the greatest recognition in their milieu (for example, tolerance, harmony, order, etc.).

It should be noted, moreover, that awareness can be clouded or distorted through the one-sided perspective that results from identification with a single pole. The poor have erroneous ideas about the rich, serious people about those who are not serious, those working in a company about the self-employed, etc. In this way, every encounter with someone from the other pole and every incident connected to that encounter will be wrongly interpreted. The person who totally identifies with one pole views everything through pole-colored glasses and, in this way, can no longer objectively recognize reality.

An additional complication is that such a person, seeking to strengthen his or her own pole, associates only with those who confirm and strengthen this essence (see Appendix: law of confirmation). Representatives of the opposite pole, or even those occupying the golden mean, may be shunned or can even become the object of hostility. In addition, all beliefs and feelings stemming from one pole, particularly an isolated one, are false (among other things, they are not reality-based). They are strongly colored due to the pole-specific glasses through which they are seen.

Viewing life through a single pole therefore leads to

1. clouded perception (due to pole-specific glasses)
2. false beliefs
3. negative assessment of the opposite pole
4. ongoing errors in interpreting the situations and events in one's own life
5. incorrect (reactive, illusive) feelings
6. manifestations of imbalance (illness, misfortune)

Because of the dogmatization of that single pole, wholeness and reality (which are bipolar) go unseen. Albert Einstein describes this situation appropriately: "You can never solve a problem on the level on which it was created."

To understand this better, let us focus on the third of the six consequences just listed above: a bipolar world produces assessments that are frequently tied to strong emotions. One pole is usually viewed as good while the other is bad and evil. Sometimes the opposite pole is even seen as pathological. The following polarities make this quite clear:

materialist	----------	esoteric
fast	----------	feast
closeness	----------	distance
tolerant	----------	intolerant
moral	----------	amoral
sophisticated	----------	vulgar
neat	----------	messy
distinguished	----------	ordinary

In some cases, the opposite pole does not even exist in fact but is seen to exist, or is simply projected onto others, based on one's own pole-specific perspective – for example, creating a bogeyman. In this way, it can only appear to a person that the other is like this.

As an example, let us look at the opposites of tolerance and intolerance. The tolerant individual stabilizes him- or herself on the one who is intolerant. If there were not so many intolerant people in the world, the tolerant individual would be alone and isolated on the tolerance pole and would have no opportunity to feel like the better person. Moreover, tolerance has natural limits. Should we tolerate everything, even that which affects our own human rights? Should we tolerate the neighbor who plays loud music, the trespasser, the thief, the employee whose lack of responsibility jeopardizes the company's existence? Are we intolerant if we report the neighbor, the trespasser, or the thief? If we fire the employee?

Furthermore, it is easy to be tolerant of situations that have no meaning to us, that do not affect our own wallet, or – as frequently happens – if we have not yet had a bad experience in a specific area. Tolerance, therefore, can also be accompanied by emotional masochism or naïveté.

Of course, the pure form of the intolerant person can also be questioned – above all, if the individual concerned is only intolerant based on prejudgments or incorrect beliefs, or even if the reason for the intolerance is only to create a bogeyman to attack, to be able to act out repressed aggressions. But we must also bear in mind that no one is born intolerant! No infant refuses to smile at a friendly face peeking into the stroller. Someone only becomes intolerant based on bad experiences, but above all out of fear – for example, the fear of being adversely affected by some action, or a worry that others may reduce one's chances in the market for a partner (same-sex competition).

Thus, a person can only be truly tolerant by tolerating those who are intolerant, by showing understanding for their formation and upbringing, for their unconscious and conscious fears. Intolerance cannot be remedied by blaming the intolerant for their attitude and condemning them as bad people, but only by listening to their arguments and bringing to light the unconscious motives that lie behind their reasoning.

This will be easier if the intolerant person perceives: here is someone who empathizes with me, who understands me, will not judge me, will not immediately call my character into question. I can be a person. In short: sometimes it is appropriate to be tolerant, especially when this involves tolerating the feelings, thoughts, and behaviors of another.

In this sense, tolerance is also the basic requirement for expanding one's own horizon, experiencing something new, growing emotionally. Such tolerance is then grounded in actual content and is not mere ideology through which we join the ranks of the noble and good.

But sometimes, when the situation demands, it can also be important to be intolerant. It is not necessary to label everything as good, to put up with everything! In such cases, it is appropriate to give expression to our 'intolerance'.

The subject of tolerance is especially important when it involve the peculiarities and habits of the opposite sex. The differences between the sexes are tied to different interests. This is unfortunately given too little consideration. Thus, some men find it difficult to understand why their partner is about to buy a new pair of shoes when she already owns over 30 pairs, or how she can spend hours on the phone with a girlfriend.

In the same manner, it is a mystery to most women that their partner cannot skip the televised sports report for fear of missing something important, or that he can spend hours in a new car showroom.

With such gender-specific peculiarities and habits, it would be out of place to show intolerance, since at heart it is otherness that makes a partner lovable. Those who are only concerned with themselves, only viewing and judging the other from the perspective of their own gender, are unrealistic and in danger of leading a lonely life.

From this excursion into the world of tolerance and intolerance, let us return to bipolarity per se. Bipolarity does not mean that the two ends of a scale represent incompatible contradictions, but rather that the two poles exist in a harmonious relationship to each other. This means that they mutually complement each other. It is central to an understanding of bipolarity to realize that a person who identifies with one pole carries the exact opposite pole within him- or herself – only that it is unconscious. Each person, therefore, can ask, "Within me, which pole is consciously at my disposal and which is only unconsciously present?" Someone who is lied to is simultaneously also the liar, lying to oneself by denying one's own individuality – for example, based on norms and ideals. It is common that a conscious lie is considered bad while an unconscious lie is good.

Even a conscious manipulation is regarded as a horrible thing, while an unconscious manipulation (such as emotional blackmail) is accepted without complaint and the 'perpetrator' protected with the excuse that "he (or she) cannot do otherwise."

Consciously placing distance between oneself and one's partner is considered cruel, but doing so unconsciously is accepted (possibly because the partner cannot spend more time at home due to career demands).

Identification with only a single pole also affects what is known as repetition compulsion: for as long as the opposite pole remains unintegrated, it will always be experienced as repetitive destiny. Confrontation of the unintegrated pole, which, as already discussed, is usually viewed as bad or evil, evokes negative feelings and a consequent predisposition to illness, especially if these negative feelings are suppressed by the affected person because of a belief system that says such feelings should not exist.

Still, it is often the case that the person's opposite pole finds a way to enter through the back door – for example, if a politically egalitarian individual behaves like King Croesus or a grande dame when staying at a hotel, or if a genteel person loses composure in key situations and is carried away with hurling vulgar and obscene comments.

There are three kinds of disposition, then, two of them vices, involving excess and deficiency respectively, and one a virtue, viz. the mean.
ARISTOTLE

The sum of both poles

The sum of both poles as a whole is greater than when they are added together in isolation. To merge both poles is not merely to compromise but rather to form a synthesis at a higher level. For example, the opposite poles of the Virgin Mary and the prostitute exist in our Western culture. The Mary pole is regarded as decent and good, while the prostitute pole is considered indecent and bad. Yet, when a woman is completely able to achieve her womanhood, she is neither Holy Virgin nor prostitute but in fact represents at a new level a completely different form of female expression. To reach this golden mean, however, she must train all her feminine capacities (motherliness, tenderness, security, psychological warmth and love, art of seduction, sexual abilities, passion, etc.) and set aside all beliefs that are specific to just one pole. It is possible to characterize such a merging of two poles as returning the respective dichotomy to unity and wholeness.

Or it can result in a synthesis:

The synthesis is the merging of the two poles at a higher level. It is also possible, however, that the synthesis will become a new thesis that results in a new antithesis. Each golden mean (which is not static but dynamic) can be precisely described in the manner of the Virgin Mary-prostitute poles already illustrated.

In this way it becomes clear that, with the golden mean, the two poles no longer truly exist. Neither pole is in fact there in its respectively typical formation. Both have merged into a synthesis, a new wholeness:

synthesis

thesis ———————|——————— antithesis

wholeness

negative pole ———————|——————— positive pole

wholeness = compensation balance synthesis
new quality
golden mean moderate reality
tension is relieved
health
start to (real) development

The prerequisite for wholeness and the result of wholeness is the modification of beliefs and attitudes. The two poles separate us from life's wholeness, while the golden mean merges us with reality, perception, authenticity – with the logos, the principle of reason and judgment.

The golden mean is not something static or something that can only be seen; rather, it is a complex new life form that has been distilled from the interactions of the two poles and that dynamically continues to differentiate and perfect itself. It could be said that this merger is a result of the other pole's process of integration.

Integration is a process through which everything finally leads to the emergence of a new identity. In other words, nothing is lost, but something new arises instead that is linked to unimagined possibilities. At the end of this process, there are no longer two separate identities struggling against each other but an expanded, consistent identity.

But why do so many people persist in their identification with a single pole? Because fear and defensiveness prevail – not only over growth and change but primarily over the development of resources and capabilities. One pole can be left behind only when we become aware of and gain knowledge about the opposite pole, when we understand the message of the opposite pole and regard that pole as a suggestion. This specifically means that a woman who closely identifies herself with the closeness pole should develop the following capacities for integrating the opposing distance pole:

- Self-sufficiency
- The capacity to engage in her own activities
- The capacity to play and have fun
- The capacity to self-actualize
- The capacity to achieve true emancipation
- The capacity to structure meaningful leisure time
- The capacity for freedom and independence
- The capacity to form and maintain friendships
- The capacity to introduce variety into her life
- The capacity to develop and act on new ideas

Development of these capacities would then result in her life becoming so varied and interesting that her need for closeness would be reduced by a healthy amount. Because of this, she would no longer suffer a lack of intimacy in her partner relationships. If, however, she exaggerates the distance pole – and this is frequently the case with newly acquired capacities – she would attract partners who cling to her, who thus behave the way she herself used to behave.

The bipolarity scale

To determine one's own position, it is important to discover and recognize one's precise location (the subjective view is often inaccurate here) on the scale between the two poles.

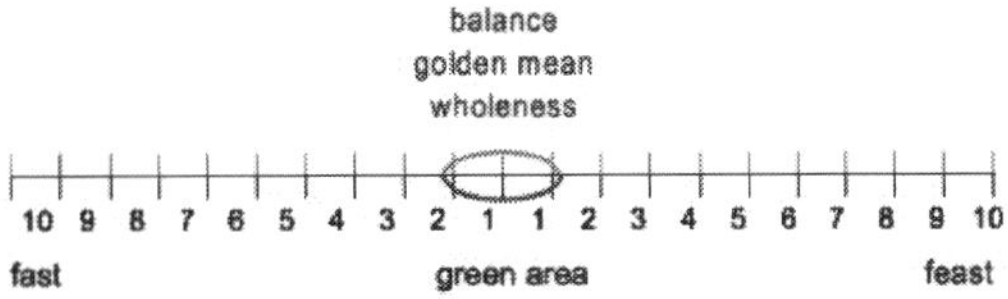

Placement outside the green area essentially signifies being out of equilibrium, a situation that leads to manifestations of imbalance (misfortune or illness). The scale also clarifies one's own relative position and the beliefs associated with that placement as well as the relative attraction of partners and acquaintances that has been achieved by such a position. In this way, the relative importance of the judgments and assessments of these partners and acquaintances will become visible. Depending on where a person stands on the scale, different assessment criteria will be applied.

In this respect, an acquaintance should not 'try on the shoe' by believing this judgment or assessment or even taking it seriously. Should this happen, it will lead to psychological pain that could be avoided by understanding that the assessment is only the result of where the other is standing and thus cannot be objectively true or generally valid.

Whoever comes to recognize this bipolarity normally poses the question: how could I have spent so much time in all these struggles, chafing against the opposite pole? How could I have believed I could change the other person in this way? It would have been possible, of course, to use one's time in a much more constructive fashion. Still, it is not useful to lose more time moaning about this situation when one can change perspective here and now. This will leave more time for the essential things in the partnership: eroticism, sex, tenderness, caring for each other, having good conversations.

Once the knowledge of bipolarity is internalized, a truly unbelievable catharsis takes place, since it will no longer be possible to label one's partner as bad, cruel, or evil. One can no longer say: You do not fit with me (any more). Since it will become clear that each of us is the opposite side of our partner's coin, this will prove that we truly fit with each other, even though it may be in ways that do not correspond to current ideals.

Why should we become upset over the other's untidiness, lies, egotism, greed, laziness etc. when all of it lives in ourselves as well, when it is only an unconscious projection of our own suppressed pole?

Many women are only concerned about their good reputation, but it is the others who become happy.
JOSEPHINE BAKER

No more lost joy and lost advantages

We have discovered how we are secretively and anonymously influenced by the unfulfilled life of the first nature with its mechanisms, capacities, and needs. Who would think that **not** having something, **not** experiencing something, can have such far-reaching consequences? Is the homeostasis of our own personality system and our own partner relationship really threatened by not having our own turf (our own space, our own room), if no skin-to-skin contact is possible, no physical pleasure is experienced, no beauty exists, we lack esthetics in our surroundings, no erotic joy is present, no passion can be felt, no freedom is permitted us, no meaning can be found in our lives?

Of course, some people succeed in fulfilling two, three, or four of these first-nature needs while believing that they do not have all the other needs or that these are not very important to them. But it is true for us all that it is precisely the neglected areas of life that particularly trouble us. Normally, however, we spend a long time unaware of destiny's negative feedback, shifting the blame to others or to misfortune instead of addressing our own unfulfilled needs.

Let us go a step further:

If the unfulfilled life of which we are unaware makes us sick and brings about setbacks such as separation and divorce, it becomes necessary to speak of lost joy and lost advantages.

So many people are unaware of their countless lost joys – physical, material, psychological, and spiritual – and, because of their inability to grasp all that they are losing, they do not even **miss** these. Then the doctor asks, almost in passing, "So what are you lacking in your life?"

The joys, advantages, and pleasures that one might have had through access to first-nature mechanisms and capacities would have provided strength for living, boosted resistance to illness, and stabilized one's own personality system and partner relationship.

How this situation can be affected when one summons the courage to confront the unfulfilled life is illustrated by the case of Sandra (39).

Sandra came to the coaching session because she was dissatisfied with her life. She had the feeling of being the stepchild of happiness, since to that point she had not experienced a fulfilling partnership. She wanted at last to have a slice of life's pie.

The first thing that Sandra learned was that she did not dress according to her type. She preferred dark, usually black clothing. She did not see herself as an attractive woman, and this negative self-perception was expressed in her low-key and not especially figure-flattering wardrobe. In addition, because of her problematic connection to her own appearance, Sandra was tense and reticent toward her sexuality.

Following several hours of coaching in which she initially struggled to reflect on her attitude toward her body, her femininity, and her sexuality, she finally began to change her inner demeanor, and this became immediately visible in her manner of dress.

The crucial moment in this process came when it was pointed out to her how little she had gained from her many years of holding onto her old conceptions and how much she had lost in the end. Because she had felt uneasy as a woman and had expressed this anxiety in her whole being, she

- depressed the mood everywhere she went;
- radiated no *joie de vivre*;
- provoked negative reactions in men resulting from her attire, which she selected based on her negative feelings. Men were virtually never willing to take her suggestions or perform acts of kindness for her;
- only attracted either female friends who were of a similarly unhappy state of mind or those who were pleased that she did not make the best of what God gave her, seeing in her no competition for the men in their lives.

What joys, advantages and pleasures had Sandra lost due to her behavior?

- Thousands of admiring gazes and compliments by men (which would have enhanced her self-concept and joy in life)
- Every man she could have gotten to know
- All the tenderness she could have received
- All the erotic joy she could have given and received
- All the good living she could have experienced with men
- All the other female friends she could have met under different conditions

- All the positive sentiments she could have felt with a different way of thinking
- All the many positive transformations of her other resources and capabilities that she had never experienced before

And who knows? Perhaps the episodes of illness that affected her life from time to time might not have occurred in the first place. Of course, it is always very difficult to prove prevention of illness, misfortune, or bad luck. But the central point is to recognize that one's own life can take a very different course when mechanisms are tolerated or cultivated than when these mechanisms cannot be integrated or set in motion in a positive way.

Many people believe they have talent for something when in fact they have none.
Many believe they have no special talent when they are indeed talented.
Many are rich in talent but too comfortable to develop, cultivate, and nurture it.
They leave it dormant.

Becoming strong together

Some people stabilize their personality system by focusing on their partner's deficiencies. In such a situation, they believe themselves to be better and more intelligent than their partner and can reinforce their own essential value based on the weaknesses of their partner. Such individuals fail to see that they too possess weaknesses and deficiencies and thus that they are in urgent (yet unconscious) need of their partner's weaknesses, which put them in a better light and offer a distraction from their own weaknesses.

There is yet another phenomenon that occurs when individuals cannot stand their partner's strengths, which are discounted since they are in unconscious rivalry with their partner or because they think they will lose power by recognizing those strengths. Cases have even been observed where one partner, hopelessly inferior in a specific area, feels not only equal but superior to the partner.

A difficulty occurs where one partner is extremely strong in a certain sphere of life, displaying exceptional talent in that area, yet shows serious weaknesses in other domains, as is often a logical consequence. This illustrates Goethe's observation: "There is strong shadow where there is much light."

In such cases, it would be very important to acknowledge and appreciate this extraordinary talent and not to insist that this person, for example, also be responsible for organizing and handling daily routines. In most cases, such a great talent also generates the means for hiring someone else (perhaps a domestic service or gardener) to take care of this part. Should this not be the case, other creative solutions can be found. It can be especially fatal to possess feelings of superiority due to the partner's weaknesses while disregarding the 'godlike' talent.

Therefore, we can establish: where a partner's weaknesses are used to compensate for one's own inadequacies, this will lead to an unhealthy atmosphere in the partnership. The partner feels ill at ease, devalued and unaccepted in his or her essence. And even one's good feelings are only an illusion since they rest on the other's deficiencies and not on one's own strengths or achievement.

The situation looks much brighter if an individual can acknowledge the partner's strengths and offer praise for these assets. It is important here not to award praise for praise's sake or flatter the partner, but only to recognize actual skills, achievements, or strengths.

Moreover, the mood is enhanced if a partner's talents, qualities, and strengths are also pointed out and emphasized in the presence of others. This should be easy if one can visualize all the ways in which the individual him- or herself can profit from these: a talent or strength can open doors to people one would otherwise never have met, economize on handyman expenses, provide security, expose new worlds, offer financial advantages, etc. It is possible to be proud of a partner whose strengths contribute new force and a higher quality of life.

Through mutual affirmation and enhancement of their qualities, both partners will be motivated and constantly renewed. In this way, joy in the relationship will continue to grow. Furthermore, the relationship becomes more relaxed, unconscious or conscious struggles end, and a truly egalitarian partnership emerges.

Questions for reflection concerning bipolarity and needs

- Which bogeymen do I have?
- With what qualities and roles (poles) do I identify?
- What beliefs have I formed regarding the poles with which I identify?
- What destiny do I attract based on such identification?
- Do I interpret all my fortunes and misfortunes through my pole-specific glasses?
- What friendships have developed based on my pole identification?
- In what areas of life does my partner represent the opposite pole?
- What learning process do I need to begin to find out more about the opposite pole?
- In what area of life have I already succeeded in finding the golden mean?
- Which three needs from the 144-need table (see appendix) have highest priority for me?
- What strategies can I pursue to fulfill my needs?
- Am I able to satisfy any of my partner's needs without having to deny myself? What are these needs?

PART FIVE
Sources of happiness

Commonalities make a relationship pleasant, but it is only the small differences that make it interesting.
CONFUCIUS

The four partner types

Following is a discussion of four different partner types: the similarity partner, the compensation partner, the complement partner, and the replacement partner. This typology is helpful in discovering which type is primarily represented by one's current partner and which type was embodied by previous partners.

It would be nice, of course, if our partner could be like ourselves, compensating and complementing us where necessary and serving as our replacement in those spheres of life where the partner enjoys a specific strength.

It is not possible to dictate that our partner exhibit similarity to us in essential respects; that is a gift. Both partners, however, can contribute in the areas of compensation and complementarity, and replacement of the other likewise is something that lies within one's power – both partners can develop and expand their respective strengths.

The best strategy is to discuss all this openly with one's partner:

How and where can we mutually compensate for and complement each other? How and where can we replace each other? To be sure, this contradicts the romantic ideal wherein happiness should occur unconsciously and almost on its own, but a relationship in which the partners proceed deliberately and strategically to achieve balance and satisfaction is more sustainable and fulfilling over time.

The similarity partner

I love the one who is like me, and I love myself in my partner.

An individual's similarity partner is one who feels, thinks, and behaves as he or she does in two or more key areas of life. Because of this similarity, the partner is perceived as very personable. Such a case is described as a 'homeopathic partner relationship': similarity can heal similarity. If each of the partners is messy, they will both be affected by this trait until one of them finally attempts to put some order to the chaos.

Relationships in which both partners are alike typically last longer than relationships where one partner represents the stark opposite of the other, since, while it is true that opposites attract, they also frequently repel each other after some time.

There is no apparent common denominator to the negative ways in which the similarity partner acts out this type, and it is important to be aware that the issue of which specific pole or qualities are considered positive or negative is a relative one. In general, it is only when partners come from the same environment that they agree on this question. In the search for a similarity partner, moreover, it is best to investigate certain interest groups or seminars. In such settings, it is possible to find a like-minded mate.

The compensation partner

I love the one who balances me.

The compensation partner is a partner who positively or negatively balances an individual in that person's own personality system. Negative compensation occurs where my partner 'balances' my shortcoming through overcompensation – such as that achieved by a compulsive talker with an inhibited speaker, a go-getter with a procrastinator, or a turf invader with a peacemaker.

Positive compensation is said to exist when poor and rich balance each other, or when a conformist is matched with a black sheep, or a helpless person pairs with a helper.

The partner who represents a positive compensation is often also the 'ideal' partner. Nevertheless, a compensation partner cannot complement or replace the other partner and is not like the other partner.

Finally, it is also possible to define a 'coincidental partner' in this light: when someone attracts a partner, it can be merely a coincidence whether this person turns out to represent similarity, compensation, complement, or replacement as a partner. It is serendipitous whether this will contribute to an individual's further development. Frequently a partner embodies not just one type, but two, three, or even all four simultaneously.

The complement partner

I love the one who complements me.

The complement partner is a person who rounds out the other in one or more spheres of life in the sense of completing a set of skills. Such complementarity was formerly accomplished through traditional role assignments: the man earned the money while the woman took care of the house and raised the children, leaving the man free for other pursuits. It was accepted that neither the man's skills nor those of the woman were sufficient to cope with the entirety of life.

Still, even today, hardly anyone would claim to be fully versed in everything or maintain that no complement is necessary. Everyone needs to be complemented in different areas of life, or perhaps needs a different kind of complement. For example, one partner may be a better negotiator, while the other is more skilled in keeping the books. One has experience dealing with bureaucracy, and the other can rapidly resolve conflicts. Where a partner cannot embody the complementarity, it becomes necessary to contract professional assistance.

Hence it is essential to distinguish between skills in the partner relationship that apply to replacement and skills that represent a complement (for example, cooking skills or handyman talents). Here an individual does not necessarily need to possess the same resources as the complement partner, while, as we will see next, it is essential for a replacement partner to have mastered the same skills.

The replacement partner

I love the one who can take my place.

A replacement partner does not mean one who can be replaced once he or she no longer satisfies the other's requirements; rather, this is one who offers the possibility of taking an individual's place in situations involving various resources and skills. This means that both the individual and the partner must have developed resources and skills in the same area, since no replacement would otherwise be possible.

If, for example, both partners possess a vivid imagination, they can exchange places with each other for further development, strengthening, energizing, and refinement of their skills or to combine in creating a product or result. If each of them spins out the other's imagination, the result may be a fantasy product that can be the basis of a theatrical script or Hollywood screenplay.

The partner relationship faces difficulty if two people come together as replacement partners in an area where the skills of one are substantially weaker than those of the other.

Spheres of life that lend themselves to a replacement partner relationship include communication, tenderness, cuddling, sexuality, intellect, and fantasy. In the sexuality arena, if one partner is a 'major leaguer', figuratively speaking, while the other has only minor-league skills, a mutually satisfying sex life is not possible. In most circumstances, the one with greater skill is brought down to the level of the less skilled partner. This is especially the case where the 'minor leaguer' judges his or her skills to be superior and is thus disinterested in overcoming any shortcomings. A partner who shows a readiness to learn can easily gain ground over time. One partner recognizes that in this specific area he or she has something to learn and will need to develop and practice the corresponding skills in the furtherance of a beautiful relationship with the other partner.

There is usually little or no discussion regarding skills and deficiencies, due to a reticence to inflict psychological pain on the partner. It is quite impossible to say to one's partner, "You are a minor leaguer in the sexual arena" or "you do this like an amateur." And, as discussed earlier, nearly everyone self-classifies as very good across almost all spheres of life due to the ubiquity of positive self-images. In sports such as soccer, tennis, or different distances of running, it can be objectively determined whether a person can keep pace with other competitors. In communication, bed, cuddling on the couch, or intellectual pursuits, such a determination is not necessarily as straightforward.

It is possible to argue that not everything is like sports and that such comparisons do not work. And yet, no one wants to communicate with a partner who performs at a substantially inferior level and with whom one has little in common to speak about. Although it is rarely admitted, these uneven levels in certain areas of life are frequently the true cause of failed relationships or separations.

The suppressed reality states:

The less skilled a person is in replacing his or her partner, the greater the danger of being abandoned by that partner.

The greater the skill level on which the replacement is based, the less likely that the partner will be left behind.

For the same reason, then, there is no need for jealousy, since decades could pass before the partner finds someone who is as good a fit. In addition, he or she is aware that there is wisdom in the saying, "Never change a winning team!"

Therefore, a partner can only achieve full performance in tandem with an appropriate (i.e., similarly skilled) partner and 'teammate'. An orchestra cannot succeed if one musician is unable to perform, plays poorly, or strikes up a different tune.

The seven partner configurations

Depending on how the four different partner types (compensation, complement, similarity, and replacement) combine as a couple, different couple configurations can result that lead respectively to different learning processes and are connected to different types of critical consciousness. In total, there are seven different couple configurations:

1. *Partners with similar weaknesses or similar deficiencies*

Here the partners are the consciousness raisers concerning their own issues, acting as a mirror. With respect to this mirror function, they need to be clear about what still must be developed in their own personality system to avoid a repetition of the problem in the future.

2. *Partners with opposite-pole issues*

Here too, this involves developing critical consciousness regarding one's own difficulties. In this case, however, the problem is not apparent in one's counterpart, as would be the case if there were a similarity of weaknesses or deficiencies, and an individual can only become aware of the issue by knowing about the bipolarity of all beings. The task is to recognize that my partner, by occupying the opposite pole, balances me in a perverted (from my own perspective) manner. An example of such a perverted compensation would be where a modest individual attracts an ostentatious partner. In such a case, the learning task is not for one to become like the other but for the two of them, working together, to find the healthy mean between the poles.

3. *My partner is weak where I unconsciously have my strength*

Let us assume that one partner has no talent for sales. By representing a negative complement, this individual acts as a consciousness raiser with respect to the other's strength. Without this example, there would have been no realization that the other partner is quite skilled in this area.

4. *My partner has a strength where I am weak*
One partner, for example, is expert in dealing with new media, while the other is very unskilled in this area. Here we can speak of a positive compensation. For the technically skilled partner, however, this weakness can also become a burden if that person is constantly called upon to assist the less capable partner.

5. *My partner is weak where I consciously have my strength*
In contrast to the partner configuration described in item 3 above, the individual is already aware of his or her own strength in this partner configuration rather than reaching this awareness through the partner's weakness. In this case, the situation is different: an individual can provide stability in the relationship because the partner is weak. Elsewhere, however, we have discussed how such a stabilization of a partner's weakness can, over time, have an unhealthy effect on the relationship. In addition, it must also be immediately clarified whether this is truly a weakness and whether the person's own strength exists in fact or only in imagination.

6. *Partners with similar strengths*
If she is a good cook and so is he, then such strengths are well matched. The law of affinity applies here. Both partners can further develop, differentiate, and enhance their talent. And they have choices: Does she cook tonight? Or does he? Or do we cook together?

7. *Partners with different strengths*
An example would be where one person excels in four different areas of life and that person's partner is particularly strong in four other areas. This is the classic sort of complement: two people complement each other so outstandingly that life becomes easier and more worthwhile for them both.

These seven configurations illustrate that everyone gets the partner you deserve and furthermore what the unconscious is attempting to do when an individual attracts a specific partner and then must come to terms with him or her. In this process, every relationship's sense of purpose is made clear. It becomes apparent that each partner needs to have some effect on the other's personality system. Each partner thus creates an opportunity to develop further, even if at the outset it does not at all look that way.

The labor of the individual for his own needs is just as much a satisfaction of the needs of others as of his own, and the satisfaction of his own needs he obtains only through the labor of others.
GEORG WILHELM FRIEDRICH HEGEL

Basic needs and subjective needs

It frequently happens that what counts in a partner is only how closely he or she fits an individual's physical, material, psychological, and intellectual ideal image and how successfully the partner can satisfy that person's needs.

The image we have of a partner is a combination of the male or female archetype and the subjective image of the man or woman. This results in the individual archetypal variation that each of us carries within ourselves.

Corresponding to the male and female archetype are basic needs that both men and women expect to be met, as well as subjective needs that emerge based on our own upbringing, individual history, and individual deficits. We expect our partner to fulfill both basic needs and subjective needs. Where this does not occur, either a budding relationship is not formed or an existing one is doomed to failure.

The example of Sandra was given to explain why it is important that a woman who yearns to be in a relationship should not allow her appearance and behavior to confuse, attack, upset, or even destroy the feminine archetype and the man's subjective image of a woman.

Since this subject is nowhere openly discussed, very few women and men are aware of its far-reaching consequences for harm. You cannot even imagine how a man is hurt when, for example, the woman appears in billowing harem trousers and green fingernails, or how a man can hurt a woman by appearing in white socks and baggy sweatpants. Many people also make the mistake of thinking that they will stay on the safe side by being fashionable and wearing whatever is 'in'.

The extent of the role external appearance can play in a relationship is illustrated by the example of Sabrina (37). Her image of a man was destroyed by her partner's outfit. Sabrina reports:

> At the start, Dan so impressed me, and I pictured myself standing at the altar with him until the day he showed up in worn sandals, red bib overalls, and the kind of grunge backpack that

> non-traditional men like to wear. I know that it is really about the person and that outward appearance should not play such a large role. But I asked myself, "What is this side of him that I have never seen before?" It struck me that he had just outed himself to me. It seemed like scales falling from my eyes: this, and not what I wanted to see, is how he truly is. It had all been just a projection on my part. My image of a man is different from how he chooses to appear. I spoke with him about it, but he said he was unwilling to deny himself and contort into some other likeness, that his attire was an expression of his political convictions that he intended to maintain. With that, I was forced to end the relationship. No doubt some other woman is his partner now – probably someone from his crowd.

When we consider the needs that a woman expects a man to fulfill and the man's own needs, it is important to distinguish between a small number of basic needs (for example, that a man should protect his family) and culturally specific needs that are considered basic because they are so widespread in the Western Hemisphere. At a recent seminar, the following needs were unanimously identified:

The 'basic needs' a man expects a woman to fulfill ...

- ☐ to bestow a sense of security and psychological warmth
- ☐ to be sensitive
- ☐ to be affectionate
- ☐ to be attractive
- ☐ to be seductive
- ☐ to know how to behave and be mannerly
- ☐ to possess sexual passion
- ☐ to care for his well-being
- ☐ to be a good mother
- ☐ to be communicative
- ☐ to be inspirational
- ☐ to be reliable

The 'basic needs' a woman expects a man to fulfill ...

- ☐ to be assertive and take initiative
- ☐ to provide protection and security for his wife and children
- ☐ to be communicative
- ☐ to provide comfort (for example, an apartment or house) and

be tender

- ☐ to be creative
- ☐ to be a good father
- ☐ to care for her well-being and that of their children
- ☐ to know how to behave and be mannerly
- ☐ to possess sexual passion
- ☐ to be spirited and sophisticated
- ☐ to be a leader
- ☐ to be reliable
- ☐ to bring variety to her life
- ☐ to disclose his past life

In the same seminar, we asked various men and women what **subjective** needs they would like to have met by their partner.

Mark (33) described his subjective image of a woman in this way:

- She is small and petite.
- She has long fingernails.
- She wears high heels.
- She has beautiful legs.
- She wears earrings.
- She walks arm in arm with me on the street.
- She caresses and fondles me for hours.
- She knows how to talk dirty

Peter (48) describes his subjective image of a woman as follows:

- She has large breasts.
- She wears low-cut dresses.
- She spends her vacation going to sporting events with me.
- She fixes a home-cooked meal every day.
- She admires my lovemaking skill.
- She wears lipstick but no makeup or perfume.
- She lets me go out often with my friends.
- She always keeps the house neat and in order.

Lisa's subjective image of a man includes the following:

- He is a good speaker.
- He is athletic.
- He likes to travel.
- He is over six feet tall.

- He earns over 100,000 euro per year.
- He is an academic.
- He likes Scandinavian design.
- He can dance tango and salsa.
- He goes with me to concerts.

Melanie, on the other hand, has a completely different subjective image of a man:

- He participates in many leisure activities with me.
- He is self-employed or in business.
- He likes to go with me to the theater and opera.
- He likes animals.
- He is a family man.
- He is close to his own family and gets along with his parents and siblings.
- He has dark hair.
- He has a weakness for modern designer furniture.
- He is vegetarian or – better still – vegan.

It is clear from these accounts how different human needs can be and, related to that, how varied the desired profiles can appear. On the one hand, this may be sobering, but on the other hand, it is apparent that no red flag of rejection is common to the entire opposite sex; instead, it is very likely that certain individuals in certain circumstances may be interested in becoming acquainted with any of these people or possibly even forming a longer-term commitment.

And as we let our own light shine, we unconsciously give other people permission to do the same.
MARIANNE WILLIAMSON

Woman and man as providers of each other's happiness

When the true needs hiding behind all the defense and adaptation mechanisms, role allocations, fixations, ideals, projections, and passing fashions are satisfied, a blissful life in companionship with one's partner becomes possible. The couple then lives out everything that a partnership has to offer: together, they experience the joys of tenderness, eroticism, sexuality, caring for each other, and intellectual growth. Both partners can then share so much power, energy, and joy with each other that their life together will be filled with love and happiness – so much joy that they can't wait to get home after work each day to experience this happiness again.

When the woman's subpersonalities of snuggle bunny, erotic seductress, sexually active woman, care provider, and source of inspiration (muse) combine with the man's subpersonalities of cuddle bear, erotic seducer, sexually active man, care provider, and intellectual initiator, it is possible to experience indescribable delights and joys. The respective energies of the woman and man can reach a synthesis, corresponding to each other and complementing each other; they will be able to stimulate, balance out, replace, enhance, positively influence, refresh, reward, and enrich each other; they can unleash synergistic processes and bring into being a new product that neither of them alone would have been able to create.

On one's own, it is impossible to experience the happiness of emotional intimacy, the cuddling and sweet nothings, the torrid eroticism and passionate nights, the happiness of caring for each other, or the mutual intellectual fertilization. The following section will illustrate how woman and man can function in a partner relationship to generate and enhance each other's happiness:

<table>
<tr><td>tender woman</td><td>↔</td><td>tender man</td></tr>
<tr><td colspan="3"><u>Result:</u> Psychological joy. The Joy of intimacy. A couple-specific psychological quality and character.</td></tr>
<tr><td>seductress</td><td>↔</td><td>seducer</td></tr>
<tr><td colspan="3"><u>Result:</u> Psychological joy. Erotic joy. A couple-specific quality and character to eroticism.</td></tr>
<tr><td>passionate woman</td><td>↔</td><td>passionate man</td></tr>
<tr><td colspan="3"><u>Result:</u> Sexual joy. A couple-specific quality and character to sex.</td></tr>
<tr><td>caring woman</td><td>↔</td><td>caring man</td></tr>
<tr><td colspan="3"><u>Result:</u> Psychological joy. The Joy of security and cohesion. The joy of mutual caring for each other. A couple-specific quality and character to living.</td></tr>
<tr><td>inspiration</td><td>↔</td><td>intellectual catalyst</td></tr>
<tr><td colspan="3"><u>Result:</u> Intellectual joy. The Joy of intimacy. A couple-specific intellectual quality and character.</td></tr>
</table>

The world will be saved by beauty.
FYODOR DOSTOYEVSKI

1. *Sources of happiness: The joys of tenderness*

The Warm Fuzzy Tale

by Claude Steiner

Once upon a time, a long time ago, there lived two happy people called Tim and Maggie with their two children, John and Lucy. To understand how happy they were you have to understand how things were in those days. You see in those happy days everyone was given a small, soft Fuzzy Bag when born. Any time a person reached into this bag they were able to pull out a Warm Fuzzy. Warm Fuzzies were very much in demand because whenever someone was given a Warm Fuzzy it made them feel warm and fuzzy all over.

In those days it was very easy to get Warm Fuzzies. Anytime that somebody felt like it, he might walk up to you and say, "I'd like to have a Warm Fuzzy." You would then reach into your bag and pull out a Fuzzy the size of a child's hand. As soon as the Fuzzy saw the light of day it would smile and blossom into a large, shaggy, Warm Fuzzy. When you laid the Warm Fuzzy on the person's head, shoulder or lap it would snuggle up and melt right against their skin and make them feel good all over.

People were always asking each other for Warm Fuzzies, and since they were always given freely, getting enough of them was never a problem. There were always plenty to go around, and so everyone was happy and felt warm and fuzzy most of the time. One day a bad witch who made salves and potions for sick people became angry because everyone was so happy and feeling good and no one was buying potions and salves. The witch was very clever and devised a very wicked plan.

One beautiful morning while Maggie was playing with her daughter the witch crept up to Tim and whispered in his ear, "See here, Tim, look at all the Fuzzies that Maggie is giving to Lucy. You know, if she keeps it up she is going to run out and then there won't be any left for you!" Tim was astonished. He turned to the witch and asked, "Do you mean to tell me that there isn't a Warm Fuzzy in our bag every time we reach into it?" And the witch answered, "No, absolutely not, and once you run out, that's it. You don't have any more." With this the witch flew away on a broom, laughing and cackling all the way. Tim took this to heart and began to notice every time Maggie gave away a Warm Fuzzy. He got very worried because he liked Maggie's Warm Fuzzies very much and did not want to give them up. He certainly did not think it was right for Maggie to be spending all her Warm Fuzzies on the children and other people. Tim began to complain or sulk when he saw Maggie giving Warm Fuzzies to somebody else, and because Maggie loved him very much, she stopped giving Warm Fuzzies to other people as often, and reserved most of them for him. The children watched this and soon began to get the idea that it was wrong to give Warm Fuzzies any time you were asked or felt like it.

They too became very careful. They would watch their parents closely and whenever they felt that one of their parents was giving too many Fuzzies to others, they felt jealous and complained and sometimes even had a tantrum. And even though they found a Warm Fuzzy every time they reached into their bag they began to feel guilty whenever they gave them away so they reached in less and less and became more and more stingy with them. Before the witch, people used to gather in groups of three, four or five, never caring too much who was giving Warm Fuzzies to whom. After the coming of the witch, people began to pair off and to reserve all their Warm Fuzzies for each other, exclusively. When people forgot to be careful and gave a Warm Fuzzy to just anybody they worried because they knew that somebody would probably resent sharing their Warm Fuzzies. People began to give less and less Warm Fuzzies, and felt less warm and less fuzzy. They began to shrivel up and, occasionally, people would even die from lack of Warm Fuzzies. People felt worse and worse and, more and more people went to the witch to buy potions and salves even though they didn't really seem to work. Well, the situation was getting very serious indeed. The bad witch who had been watching all of this didn't really want the people to die (since dead people couldn't buy his salves and potions), so a new plan was devised. Everyone was given, free of charge, a bag that was very similar to the Fuzzy Bag except that this one was cold while the Fuzzy Bag was warm. Inside of the witch's bag were Cold Pricklies. These Cold Pricklies did not make people feel warm and fuzzy; in fact, they made them feel cold and prickly instead.

But the Cold Pricklies were better than nothing and they did prevent peoples' backs from shriveling up. So, from then on, when somebody asked for a Warm Fuzzy, people who were worried about depleting their supply would say, "I can't give you a Warm Fuzzy, but would you like a Cold Prickly instead?" Sometimes, two people would walk up to each other, thinking they maybe they could get a Warm Fuzzy this time, but one of them would change his mind and they would wind up giving each other Cold Pricklies instead. So, the end result was that people were not dying anymore but a lot of people were very unhappy and feeling very cold and prickly indeed. The situation got very complicated since the coming of the witch because there were fewer and fewer Warm Fuzzies around and Warm Fuzzies which used to be free as air, became extremely valuable. This caused people to do all sorts of things in order to get Warm Fuzzies.

People who could not find a generous partner had to buy their Warm Fuzzies and had to work long hours to earn the money. Some people became 'popular' and got a lot of Warm Fuzzies without having to give any back. These people would then sell their Warm Fuzzies to people who were 'unpopular' and needed them to feel that life was worth living. Another thing which happened was that some people would take Cold Pricklies--which were everywhere and freely available-and coated them white and fluffy so that they almost looked like Warm Fuzzies. These fake Warm Fuzzies were really Plastic Fuzzies, and they caused additional problems. For instance, two or more people would get together and freely give each other Plastic Fuzzies. They expected to feel good, but they came away feeling bad instead. People got very confused never realizing that their cold, prickly feelings were because they had been given a lot of Plastic Fuzzies. So the situation was very, very dismal and it all started because of the coming of the witch who made people believe that some day, when least expected, they might reach into their Warm Fuzzy Bag and find no more.

Not long ago, a lovely, strong woman with big hips came to this unhappy land. She seemed not to have heard about the bad witch and was not worried about running out of Warm Fuzzies. She gave them out freely, even when not asked. They called her the Hip Woman and disapproved of her because she was giving the children the idea that they should not worry about running out of Warm Fuzzies.

The children liked her very much because they felt good around her and they began to follow her example giving out Warm Fuzzies whenever they felt like it. This made the grownups very worried. To protect the children from depleting their supplies of Warm Fuzzies they passed a law. The law made it a criminal offense to give out Warm Fuzzies in a reckless man-

> ner or without a license. Many children, however, seemed not to care; and in spite of the law they continued to give each other Warm Fuzzies whenever they felt like it and always when asked. Because they were many, many children, almost as many as grownups, it began to look as if maybe they would have their way.
>
> As of now it is hard to say what will happen. Will the grownups' laws stop the recklessness of the children? Are the grownups going to join with the Hip Woman and the children in taking a chance that there will always be as many Warm Fuzzies as needed? Will they remember the days their children are trying to bring back when Warm Fuzzies were abundant because people gave them away freely? The struggle spread all over the land and is probably going on right where you live. If you want to, and I hope you do, you can join by freely giving and asking for Warm Fuzzies and being as loving and healthy as you can.

This story by Claude Steiner symbolically and analogically represents the dearth of care and tenderness in our society. The impact of such scarcity is made starkly clear by hospitalism.

All the negative physical and psychological side effects of a stay in a hospital or clinic are called 'hospitalism'. This concept also includes the deficient care and unloving treatment of infants and children. The pioneering research of the psychoanalyst René A. Spitz in this area is well known. The vivid images documented in his films on the psychological suffering of abandoned infants triggered deep consternation even among professionals. Spitz and his colleagues observed small children who had been separated from their mothers by the age of three months. The infants remained in a foundling house, where they were provided with hygienic conditions and medical care in every respect. Since there was only one nurse for between eight and twelve infants, however, they gradually developed 'psychological starvation.' According to Spitz, "They received approximately one tenth the amount of emotional attention they would have enjoyed in a normal mother-child relationship." Following separation from their mothers, the children initially displayed symptoms of advanced decline. After three months, they exhibited serious developmental lags. Once again, from Spitz: "The retardation of motor skills was fully in evidence; the children were completely passive; they lay on their backs in their cribs. They did not achieve the level of motor development necessary to turn onto their stomachs. Their facial expressions were blank and often vacuous, their eye coordination declined. The children's test performance revealed progressive shortfall. The average developmental quotient by the end of their second year of life was just 45 percent of their age norm. Of 91 children we initially observed in the foundling house, 34 had died by the end of the second year, while 57 were still living."

In a figurative sense, however, we are basically dealing with a widespread 'adult hospitalism'. What is the origin of this 'illness'? How can this be if a person has never been hospitalized as either a child or an adult? The reasons can be manifold, and they lie concealed in the personal history of our childhood: the mother punishes the child who misbehaves or fails to live up to her expectations by withholding tenderness. A new baby in the family draws all the attention, or the parents decide that a child over six years old no longer needs tenderness and affection.

In fact, we all need to be hugged and caressed for our entire life – initially by parents, then by a peer group, and finally by our partner. That is what happens externally. It is also important to consider what takes place internally, however. The parent-child relationship remains in the psyche of every individual for a lifetime.

As indicated above, the point is that a person becomes his or her true father and true mother, but also that, acting as the parents of the inner child within, this individual also constantly looks after, takes care of, and nurtures the child within his or her own partner.

Keep in mind that every inner child clamors daily for attention, tenderness, and love. Most people, however, try to ignore, repress, and camouflage this inner cry. For all these reasons and more, our society reflects an unimaginable lack of tenderness. In our workshops on tenderness, this scarcity is quite openly on display: for the first time, in a protected space, many participants have the courage to confess their neediness and demand affection. Some of them simply want to be held in someone's arms for five or ten minutes.

There are people, however, who truly have a natural talent for providing tenderness. A woman can be a 'queen of tenderness'; a man can be the 'king of tenderness.' These individuals instinctively sense how they can pamper their partner with tenderness and love. They are aware of the almost endless positions and varieties of tenderness (in one workshop, participants discovered 127 tenderness varieties). There are more tenderness positions than sex positions. Above all, it is the subtle nuances of tenderness that frequently have the greatest effect here.

It is especially wonderful when a person can interact with his or her partner as with an infant, holding the partner's head, rocking the partner, drawing him or her close, giving kisses, whispering words of love in the partner's ear. It is essential to provide a feeling of safety and security – and perhaps be allowed to drift off to peaceful sleep.

Oxytocin, known as the snuggling or bonding hormone, can also assist in overcoming anxieties. This was revealed in a study by researchers at the University of Bonn. They found that oxytocin, which promotes bonding between partners or in a mother-child relationship, helps individuals to leave their anxieties behind and 'over-write' them in their memory.

Even if there is not much going on erotically or sexually in a relationship, with little mutual caring and harmony, regularly devoting evenings to cuddling can, on its own, reinforce the relationship and, in this way, bring a great deal of happiness. During cuddling, all cares and concerns are forgotten, and many everyday problems become less important. It is as if one were in another world where time and space are no longer recalled.

One senses an overflowing of psychological warmth, charging one's emotional battery, experiencing the emergence of happiness and contentment. It is like discovering paradise.

This all shows what true love means.

True love signifies loving someone despite all masks and roles. It means recognizing and accepting the person's true nature.

This true essence in another can only be perceived, however, by first tapping into one's own true essence, true nature, one's own world of emotions, the 'animal' and shadow within. It is only once we become aware of everything harbored inside us that we can show understanding for our partner's inner makeup. Only then can we experience the other person: whether he or she is full of prejudice and intolerance, mired in financial difficulty, or inclined to be promiscuous. Someone who truly loves will want to know why the other is narrow-minded, penniless, or constantly unfaithful, refraining from devaluing or passing judgement, seeking to comprehend how the partner truly feels and thinks, what sorts of influences were present in childhood, and what fears and protective postures were carried into adulthood.

True love is expressed physically, psychologically, and spiritually. To give genuine love to another means feeling the urge to share physical, psychological, and spiritual joy and accepting, embracing, and providing security for the inner child – the little boy or girl – within one's partner. Only in this way can true trust, true intimacy – and true love – grow.

To increase the motivation to build the competence to offer tenderness, we provide a short list below of the negative consequences that usually result in a partner relationship when this resource is not present.

When tenderness is lacking in the personality of a woman or man:

- there is no emotional intimacy
- the partner is not compensated emotionally
- the partner does not feel accepted
- the partner feels unsafe
- the bonding hormone oxytocin is not released
- the partner cannot replenish psychological energy
- the partner experiences no psychological joy
- the partner is dissatisfied
- since psychological energy is not reciprocated, it is transformed into aggression, anger, fanaticism, or illness
- the security deficits need to be compensated in another area of life
- a tendency toward craving develops

Here as well as in the following four sources of happiness, it is important to make clear that something serious is lacking in the partner. As a result, the partner is limited in wholeness and weakened in capacity for bonding. When a woman has not yet developed a certain subpersonality, letting it lie fallow, her partner cannot experience being the counterpart to it; in turn, when a subpersonality is lacking in the man, then she cannot become its opposite number. Wherever the foil is missing, it becomes impossible to do anything with one's own resources, however well developed these may be. It is as if these resources did not exist at all. The result is a manifestation of imbalance. Every obstruction of a resource demonstrates how the insufficient investment of resources also brings about far-reaching consequences for the self. There is no other way to receive what a person very strongly wants – or urgently needs – to have.

The erotic... belongs on the one hand to the original drive nature of man...On the other hand, it is related to the highest forms of the spirit. It only thrives when spirit and drive are in the right harmony.
CARL JUNG

2. Sources of happiness: The joys of eroticism

In eroticism, desire and feeling *consciously* arrive at a synthesis. 'Consciously' means that a person reflects on his or her specific physical and emotional nature, develops and differentiates these resources further, and, in doing so, consciously applies them. Eroticism can also be understood as an expanded sexuality in which one has learned how to adjust to a partner's individual physical and emotional nature, where attention is given to action and reaction, and the laws of Eros are applied. Eroticism is an art that must be learned. By no means are all people capable of creating a sweet and pleasing atmosphere conducive for the giving and receiving of joy. Two people who have mastered the art of eroticism can spend a weekend full of love and happiness. They constantly conceive new ideas for pleasing each other and arousing erotic feelings. Still, eroticism requires 'cleansed' feelings. Depression, fear, inhibitions, feelings of guilt, etc. restrict the erotic adventure, as do cramped living conditions, illness, forced ritual activities, bias, and much more.

The sensual person can create an erotic mood through physical and emotional expression; attractive, tasteful clothing; the home environment; the preparation of stimulating dishes... everything is set up for the pleasure of his or her own eyes, ears, nose, palate, body, and spirit as well the partner's senses, body and spirit.

Both internally and externally, eroticism offers freedom from convention and grants abundance, release, and pleasure. In contract to superficial opulence, an erotic life does not need to involve heavy cost. Frequently, greater effect can be achieved at low expense than from expensive wardrobes or magnificent surroundings.

To be sensual does not mean, as is so often erroneously assumed, being in a state of constant arousal. Rather, eroticism is an expression of balance, harmony, happiness, joy, and contentment. Life takes place in a satisfying atmosphere. People indulge themselves. Such good living assumes, however, that old needs have been fulfilled by this point. Ongoing concerns over shelter or employment, to cite two examples, create poor conditions for eroticism to flower. This means, therefore, that all human development stages characterized by illness, war, and want – situations where people person are constrained to fight to secure their existence – are inimical to the growth of eroticism.

Where material security (not to be confused with wealth) is assured, it is possible to refine one's instincts and feelings, not through sublimation in the Freudian sense of defense and adaptation mechanisms but through the enhancement of physical and spiritual love at new levels and in a wide variety of nuances. This advanced development means that eroticism becomes a specifically human phenomenon. This type of uncoupling from animal instincts is fundamentally different from the perspective of those who deny animal urges, who employ asceticism and suppression to overcome the 'animal' within themselves. In such a new sensuality, nature and culture are harmoniously combined. Vital eroticism is an element of a new humanity.

In Greek mythology, Aphrodite is the goddess of love, beauty, pleasure, and eroticism.

She wears a magical saltire band around her body: all her magical powers are contained in this strap.

"Love and longing and lovers' chats that so often charmed sensible men" is the refrain of an old anthem.

From this perspective, eroticism is the domain of the woman. She creates the erotic mood that is the source of so much joy and happiness.

At heart, she is the active partner in an erotic encounter, and the man the reactive partner. His reactions, however, play a key role in affecting the woman's actions. If he fails to respond to her, she becomes frustrated and feels undesired.

Through his reactions, the man can evoke or reinforce specific ideas and behaviors in the woman. If he is enthusiastic about her erotic vibrancy and seductiveness, this excitement strengthens her self-confidence and vitality.

It is important, however, that the man also contribute to the sensual mood – for example, through carefully selected attire, through hygiene and cleanliness, or by eliminating any distractions and resolving conflicts. He can create erotic surroundings. If the man fails to do his part, eroticism cannot become a celebration.

In the chapter on lost joy and lost advantages, we discussed the case of Sandra, whose drab attire stifled any erotic attraction. Now we want to take a closer look at the phenomenon of erotic attraction by examining the case of Ellen.

Ellen lived with Michael for six years. They got along splendidly with each other – except when it came to eroticism. "Michael insisted that I play a very specific role leading up to the sex act," she reported. "Once he wanted me to come into the bedroom wearing nothing but a string of pearls and high heels. On another occasion, he wanted me to serve him dinner wearing lingerie, and yet another time he wanted me to talk dirty to him. In the face of demands like these, I constantly feel pressured by him. I often simply refuse to do these things. Then I feel stupid. And if, to keep peace in the house, I ever play these roles for him, then the erotic element seems so forced and artificial to me.

I would like to see us develop a fulfilling sexual relationship without such a song and dance. I sometimes ask myself why Michael needs these things at all."

Under the law of balance (see upcoming chapter), the partner feeling pressure is the one who fails to cultivate a personalized imagination, who develops no model or program of his or her own. Since Ellen has not created her own program, she is confronted with Michael's expectations. Her partner's imagination creates stress for her because it is his fantasy, not hers. In this way, Ellen is compensated by the opposite pole, affected by that which she lacks. It can also be explained this way: Within herself, she has not developed her erotic character – she has repressed it. For this reason, her own repression comes out in the external world as pressure from her partner. The partner's pressure thus serves as an *intensifier* – through it, she becomes even less able to discover her erotic character. Yet that which she experiences as external pressure is in fact nothing other than her own internal pressure. Thus, it is not as effective to resist the external pressure. Such an undertaking would be virtually a Sisyphean task. On the contrary, it would be much better for her to develop her *own* imagination, a program of her own featuring the way she herself would fashion eroticism, what would be enjoyable for her. In this manner, she would have something to contribute to the balance, something to offer. As a result, it would be possible to come to terms with her partner, coordinate with him, and thus accommodate each other.

Since Ellen devalues her partner for his erotic imagination, however, it also becomes necessary to clarify at the outset where the boundaries will be between normal sexuality and sexual deviancy. A sexual inclination toward individual parts of the body, lingerie, articles of clothing, shoes, and other objects is generally regarded as within the normal range of sexuality. If the fetish is linked to a living human being and the inanimate object is not the sole object of sexual desire, no abnormal sexual behavior is present. Fundamentally, all men are fetishists (fetishism rarely occurs in women). Almost every man has a predilection for certain external objects or items of apparel, starting with high heels, anklets, brassieres, fishnet stockings, garter-less stockings, garter belts, corsets, or red-polished fingernails and toenails. At the University of Bretagne-Sud in France, there is an interesting study of high heels directed by Nicolas Guegén that shows that men's willingness to help women is positively correlated with the height of their heeled shoes. In contrast, however, heel height has no effect on women's helpfulness.

In a final experiment, Guegén found that men in a bar more readily approached women wearing high heels. "The height of a woman's heels has a strong influence on male behavior," he concludes. In his opinion, this indicates how strongly men focus on physical attributes in judging or interacting with women.

The most pronounced male fetishism, however, occurs in the category of fetishes for bodily features – in other words, a fondness for a specific area of a woman's body. This frequently involves specific shapes of a woman's buttocks (apple, pear, tomato, potato, or nectarine) or breasts.

These constitute an unconscious symbolic compensation. It is important to distinguish between a man's symbolic compensation and that of a woman. In this area, a woman's specific bodily attributes can become a symbolic representation of what the man is lacking. For example, if a man experienced little psychological warmth and security in childhood, he may prefer women with large breasts. If he had difficulty establishing his place in the family as a child, or if he was constantly devalued, a proclivity for women with pronounced buttocks is the result. The buttocks, otherwise called the rear, butt, or bottom among countless other designations, represent seating oneself, alighting, being firmly ensconced, having security. This is fundamentally about the feeling of merit or value.

The significance of female breasts for a man frequently corresponds to the importance of a beautiful house or apartment for a woman – a place where she can feel cozy and secure. And the part played for men by the female buttocks is possibly equivalent to the role of a man's status and possessions for women.

As we have seen above, breasts and buttocks are not essential to the mission of charming a man. A woman can employ erotic stimulation to get to know men. If a woman wishes, she can make skillful use of stimuli such as miniskirts or red fingernails to attract all sorts of men, depending on their respective likings. The difficulty, however, lies in recognizing the right time and moment for such devices. We have seen that the erotic arts involve a good deal of empathy, knowledge of the opposite sex, and acting ability, a considerable amount of good will and love toward the partner.

It is important that both women and men develop their own highly personal erotic character and that they become attuned to the erotic character of their partner.

At the outset, we can reflect on the way we want to express our erotic character.

Since eroticism involves deeply felt sensual pleasure, which is the pleasure of seeing, hearing, smelling, tasting, and touching, it is possible to develop ideas and notions of how best to express one's physical and mental distinctiveness – one's bodily and emotional sensations – while at the same time producing in one's partner sensations of being excited, seduced, pleasured, indulged, and loved.

Visual stimulation: for instance, if a woman is in an erotic mood and knows that men are especially susceptible to visual stimuli, she can take pleasure in displaying her body and using makeup, certain articles of clothing, or jewelry to bring out her best features. In doing so, it is important for her to be aware that the color, cut, and shape of each piece of clothing or each jewelry item she selects **will bring out different feelings in the opposite sex**. It is a fact that even her choice of earrings can conjure up a different mood each time she enters a room. It makes a difference whether these are pearl earrings or creole earrings, whether they feature stars or hearts. Which of them will trigger in her partner a happy frame of mind? Which will prompt approval, affection, feelings of love, erotic stimulation, or the desire to protect, embrace, or kiss her? These subtle nuances that can be provoked by a woman's outfit are comparable to flowers, the stars, or the earth.

A tulip produces a different feeling in the observer than does a rose or daisy. The question is therefore not only what the woman in question prefers, what suits her the best, but also what effect her choice of makeup, dress, and appearance will have on the opposite sex.

For most men, it is always pleasing when their partner emphasizes her feminine side. As Goethe expresses it, "The eternal feminine draws us ever upward."

Acoustical stimulation: a man can display his feelings, for example, by whispering tender, loving, or arousing words in her ear, in this way enticing her, exciting her, conveying safety and security, triggering feelings of joy and happiness. A key condition, however, is that the man must truly feel what his words express – in other words, that content and form are coordinated. In addition, it is good to introduce variety into the discourse by expanding one's vocabulary, changing up the words, imagining new possibilities. Merely repeating the three words "I love you" can give rise to boredom or a certain dullness.

Olfactory stimulation: every human being has a highly specific scent. If our sense of smell were not so atrophied, we would have the capacity to 'sniff out' suitable partners from a distance. There is an old saying: "That really gets up my nose." Here the difficulty lies primarily in the fact that a person's own scent is constantly being altered through unhealthy living, poor nutrition, and estranged working relationships as well as all manner of perfumes and *eaux de toilette*. Regarding this, Otto Mainzer maintains: "Erotic perception and the sweet scent of the individual are masked by modern morals. Frequently, this process goes hand in hand with supposed hygienic requirements that camouflage puritanical taboos and lead to a seemingly reasonable kind of coercion that mandates daily showering and use of deodorant. If all erotic signals between two lovers are disabled by modern, gender-alien routines, it becomes even more difficult for spruced-up, certified-germ-free bipeds whose banal daily encounters are void of all exercise of personality to restore any sort of spontaneity."

The challenge is therefore to recover one's own scent through breaking down alienation – by experiencing sun, wind, water, and nature and incorporating a natural diet that will alter the scent of one's perspiration because the body will have less need to expel toxic substances – and above all through more physical and psychological love, which releases different hormones.

Gustatory stimulation: What has been said regarding the sense of smell applies equally to the sense of taste. Taste buds are often perverted through excessive use of tobacco and alcohol as well as by poor nutrition. Partner selection can also occur through an undistorted sense of taste. For example, since every kiss tastes different, a good way for a person engaged in the search for a partner to find the one that fits his or her 'taste' is by kissing many candidates.

When the concept of taste is understood in its broader sense, then it becomes extremely important that a person learn how to create an atmosphere that is consistent with the partner's tastes, where both partners can feel comfortable. There is so much that can enhance the erotic effect: appetizing foods, a romantic garden, cozy surroundings, soft lighting, beautiful music, and a great deal more. An 'unerotic' environment has spoiled many a rendezvous or substantially diminished the quality of such encounters.

When eroticism is lacking in the personality of a woman or man:

- there is no erotic stimulation
- joy of life is reduced
- the partner is less often in a good mood and does not look forward to spending happy evenings together
- the partner's feelings of love diminish
- the partner displays less desire
- the partner's urge to show tenderness, engage in sex, and care for the other is reduced (effects on other areas of life)
- the partner's quality of life is diminished
- the partner displays less generosity and gift-giving
- the partner does not feel valued
- the partner seeks erotic stimulation elsewhere
- the partner is not compensated and must find compensation in other areas of life

On the path to seventh heaven, many people become stuck in the sixth.
HELGA SCHÄFERLING

3. Sources of happiness: The joys of sex

We understand the sex drive as the dynamic, stimulating element that 'drives' or 'energizes' the organism to engage in purposeful behavior to satisfy a need. The sex drive is an innate or primary drive. It can be present at abnormally powerful or reduced levels, or it can be qualitatively enhanced. According to Sigmund Freud, every drive has its origin in a physical arousal that provokes excitement in the drive.

In its most basic sense, sexuality is understood as the sex act itself. It consists of foreplay, coitus in varied positions, and orgasm.

Despite emancipation and apparent sexual permissiveness, the biggest obstacle to sexual fulfillment remains traditional sexual morality.

Many people hold that traditional ways are natural or normal, while anything that deviates from this standard is perverse.

It is true, however, that such standards, so frequently portrayed as irrevocable, have in fact constantly changed over time and are substantially different across cultures. Furthermore, a standard is specific to a period, a setting, a culture – even to families and individuals. For example: the youngest sibling in a family generally enjoys greater sexual freedom than did the first-born child. Thus, the standard is not a yardstick for measuring what is natural and what is not. It merely symbolizes a society's – or an individual's – level of development and awareness.

Tightly interwoven with these standards are of course the so-called perversions (deviations from the norm). Every standard creates its own perversions and affects others. Viewed in this manner, perversions are the consequences of and reactions to specific norms. To be perverted effectively means to be 'twisted', and the term implies the suspicion that most standards and ideals regarding sexual behavior are in fact twisted – i.e., that they are against human nature and thus constitute a distortion of natural sexuality.

This is because, if the prevailing standards and ideals were indeed natural, no perversion of them would ensue. The expressions 'normal' and 'perverse' would, on their own, cease to have meaning.

A conscious couple relationship, rather than sticking to the old role assignments, can be built on personal characteristics, individual aptitudes, and resources, on the partner's possibilities and desires.

It is no different with sexuality. Such a conscious form of partner relationship is not simply devoted to needs satisfaction: in this case, sexuality includes the attempt by both partners to achieve synthesis. The partner's body becomes a territory to be explored. And if success does not come immediately, this does not call for giving up and immediately moving on to the next partner but instead for altering the form or pattern of manual, oral, or genital stimulation and expanding one's own sexual program. A different way of holding the partner, a new angle that can produce stimulation, another pressure point or manner of caressing, another form of tongue play, or a different rhythm can lead to maximum arousal. It is especially important to give attention to these techniques when a long-time relationship ends and a new partner enters the stage of one's life. When this occurs, one frequently learns that what drove the earlier partner wild with desire leaves the new one cold.

In this respect, any specific sexual behavior cannot be wholly transferred into a new relationship. The new partner is different, has other sexual preferences, a different physical and sexual character, has other sensitive erogenous zones, other sexual fantasies, and a different set of sexual behaviors.

Consequently, action and reaction need to be recalibrated; timing and coordination must be in sync.

This refinement is often a lengthy process that can only succeed if neither partner becomes impatient, if no feelings of shame, fear, or insecurity arise.

Sound is especially significant during the sexual union. There are couples who have sex in total silence. In such surroundings, sounds of delight and wantonness spark unimagined passions. The more one partner emerges, the more the other gives. If, on occasion, the pre-coital setting contributes to heightened inhibition and consequently a reduced sexual experience, then the subsequent pleasure of one partner will be enhanced by that of the other.

When sexual vigor (passion) is lacking in the personality of a woman or man:

- the partner feels sexually uncompensated
- the partner is insufficiently aroused and must forgo sexual pleasure

- the partner scales back his or her courting behavior
- the partner is forced to repress the sexual drive
- the partner somaticizes the repressed drive in the form of headaches or abdominal discomfort
- the partner becomes hormonally imbalanced (too little secretion of testosterone or estrogen)
- the partner attempts to satisfy the sexual drive in other ways
- the partner is not energetically charged
- the partner's zest for life is reduced
- the partner becomes unhappy
- sexual intimacy does not take place
- the partner sublimates his or her sexual drive
- the partner limits his or her investment of time and energy to other areas of the relationship
- the partner's generosity and tolerance wanes
- the partner becomes distant or ends the relationship

The more joy we create for others, the more joy comes back into our heart.
ANONYMOUS

4. Sources of happiness: The joys of mutual caring

The secret recipe for a good partner relationship is this: each of the partners ensures the well-being of both. Each is gratified to know that the partner is there in the difficult situations, that each partner can be counted on not to let the other down, that each will assist when things go wrong, and that each protects the other.

Each partner ensures that the other does not want for anything, that the basic needs of food, clothing, and shelter are met, and that someone is there in case of illness, caring for the other and supporting the healing process.

To a certain extent, mutual caring represents an extension of the joy of tenderness. If the latter means that partners are father, mother, and child to each other on a psychological level, now the duty involves caring for each other on a material level.

These gestures of attention and psychological love are an expression of the tenderness that each feels for the other. They can include the bringing of things: flowers, a newspaper article that will interest the other, a book on a specific subject, a tasty treat, or anything else likely to produce joy in the other partner.

It is especially important in this connection to allow a partner to enjoy freedom of independent action – whether that means going out with friends, enjoying athletic pursuits, engaging in a hobby, or visiting any children from a previous alliance.

In a partner relationship, it is necessary to ensure that the man can be a man and that the woman can be a woman. And it is a matter of strengthening the development of the partner's physical, emotional, and intellectual potential, encouraging and supporting the actualization of the partner's resources.

In a broader sense, caring for a partner means not only having understanding but also making sure that the partner is compensated and happy.

Each partner has the right to achieve balance! This is the only way to allow the partner to lead his or her own life – an action that, in the end, also makes a favorable impact on the existing couple relationship.

A requirement for doing so, however, is to be sufficiently advanced in one's own personality development that no feelings of jealousy emerge. And it is also unproductive – as so often happens – whenever one partner sees the other as a rival. In such cases, it is advisable to call to mind the following: we are not in competition with each other to see who is smarter, better, or more successful; rather, we are building a team together that can hold its own in the world and benefit from each team member.

When caring is lacking in the personality of a woman or man:

- the partner feels insecure in the relationship
- the partner has no 'true' home
- the partner feels unappreciated and unimportant
- the partner feels less invested in maintaining the bond
- the partner lacks a counterpart for his or her role
- the partner feels overwhelmed (since it is necessary to take on the other's role in addition to his or her own)
- an unequal give-and-take develops that must be compensated elsewhere
- the partner feels abandoned and reacts with illness, depression, or cravings
- the partner notices how his or her own feelings of love are waning

A substance can exist without thinking, but thinking cannot exist without substance.
GOTTFRIED LEIBNIZ

5. Sources of happiness: The intellectual joys

The most important requirement for intellectual joy in a relationship is for both partners to have sufficiently developed the ability to communicate. The following overview of the reasons for the widespread lack of communication ability underscores why it so rarely occurs that two people are simply able to communicate with each other.

Possible causes of a lack of communication ability	
Lack of intelligence	Lack of education
Lack of information	Assumption of the parent or child role
Lack of curiosity about life	Ignorance
Lack of capacity for logical thinking	Resistance and defensiveness, intolerance
Lack of listening ability	Emotional chaos
External determination	Megalomania
Manipulation	Contrarian attitudes
Lack of analytical capacity	Inability to view something from a bird-eye perspective
Dogmatism	Bogeymen
Commitment to ideas	Lack of sense of reality
Paranoid thinking	Demand to lead the conversation
Lack of interest	Obsession with detail
Neutrality (not taking a stand)	Tendency toward projection
Lack of empathy	Lack of fantasy
Tendency to talk too much	Trust in an authority or guru
Lack of ability to deviate	Lack of self-reflection and from structure
Tendency toward destructive criticism	Dogmatism

We can see how difficult it is to carry on communication that is adequate to reality at an 'adult' level. Different perceptions can be attributed to the personality characteristics of the sender (the one sending a message in oral or written form) or the receiver (the one who receives a message) – i.e., based on feelings, subjective perceptions, attitudes, world views, awareness, etc. Moreover, difficulties in communicating can arise from the nature of the sender-receiver relationship, the sender's intentions, the sender's encoding ability, the medium (the channel or the chosen means of communication), and the receiver's decoding ability – that is, the receiver's ability to be accurate in interpreting the sender's message. In addition, it is important to successful communication that each partner possess his or her own information and the willingness to pass it on. The partner's information broadens the other's horizons. The maxim is: we are stronger together, since together we have more information at our disposal than we would as individuals.

A person who is intellectually vibrant has no end of interests. Such a person wants to know how the human body is constructed and how it works (medicine) and what legitimacies play a role in the psyche (psychology); wants to explore the types of human coexistence (sociology), to learn about vital processes in nature (biology) and the relationship of living things to their environment (ecology). He or she is concerned with education, construction, and habitation; with literature, management, and success; with the science and lore on destiny; with partner and relationship skills; with astronomy; with various world views; with philosophies... With such diverse interests, the house never falls in on such a person, who is also never bored since there is enough to do to last many lifetimes! From this spectrum of intellectual interests, let us simply select medicine: even a person who studies only this field for fifty, sixty, or even seventy years will never come close to achieving perfection in this discipline. There are always new doctrines, new research results, new ideas, new therapies!

So: what is the current situation regarding the partner relationship? Through learning about the four types of unconscious, the six images in the psyche of the man and woman, and bipolarity and beliefs about it, it becomes easier for partners to carry on an intellectual discussion with each other, since in this way the intellectual walls can be torn down that would otherwise prevent successful communication right from the outset.

Since an enormous intellectual potential inhabits every individual, each day can lead to new realizations. Each partner constantly forms new ideas, becomes aware of new things, or discovers new information.

The most rewarding aspect is when partners can stimulate each other intellectually – when one reads an interesting article or a book that is intellectually enriching, or attends an educational event that provides new insights, and then shares all this later at home. The partner comments, offers constructive criticism, or extends the thought from the vantage of his or her own conceptual world and fantasy. The two of them engage in mutual intellectual stimulation that is highly enjoyable and that also bonds them as a couple. Car journeys, evenings, and weekends become more interesting. They experience intellectual adventures that they would never want to do without.

Particularly exciting are conversations on topics where the partners have contrary viewpoints. By accepting the challenge and communicating fairly with one's partner, it is possible to get closer to reality and truth than in situations where both are already in full agreement with each other.

It is also advisable to take notes at such times and possibly discuss these subjects with friends. In this way, a conversation can go from narration culture (for example, where one went on vacation or what the food was like there) to issue culture, which, in the end, inspires participants intellectually and provides them with much more enjoyment than if only one of them has the pleasure of relating experiences while the others become bored and start to nod off.

So it raises the mood in a relationship enormously, if you enrich each other spiritually. But what happens if a husband and wife can`t be sources of inspiration for each other? If the woman, specifically with her partner, can`t develop or use her personality as a muse, or if the man does not appear as a spiritual impulse for his partner?

When the ability to stimulate intellectually is lacking in the personality of a woman or man:

- there is no joy of conversation; communication is poor or scant
- no intellectual joy emerges, and thus less feeling of belonging

- pain is felt because there is no intellectual agreement
- there is no development of intellectual vibrancy or growth
- no intellectual discoveries or adventures are possible
- communication with the partner signifies wasted time and self-denial
- horizons are not broadened
- consciousness is not awakened within the partner relationship
- no new common realizations are possible
- togetherness becomes boring beyond a certain point

Happiness is everywhere. It only has to be found.
CONFUCIUS

The 15 joys

Even if it is only possible to achieve two of the five joys, this still represents an enormous improvement in the quality of life. Just imagine how reinforcing and strengthening it would be if three, four, or all five sources of happiness were at one's disposal.

In addition, it must be borne in mind that each joy affects other resources and subpersonalities. Every resource constantly interacts with other resources! Cuddling and tenderness have a positive influence on eroticism, sexuality, and mutual caring – eroticism supports the urge to convey tenderness, the desire for sexual union, and the need to care for and bestow gifts on the partner.

Furthermore: the intellectual joys stimulate all other parts of the personality, allowing for greater experimentation and variety.

It is also interesting in this connection that every relationship is differently weighted: one couple places greater emphasis on cuddling and caring for each other, while another stresses eroticism and sex, and a third couple focuses more on cuddling and intellectual exchange. The opportunity for extending the repertoire to involve all five joys is always there.

In this way, it is basically very easy to maintain the completely fulfilling relationship we deserve if both partners are working toward their own individual AND joint happiness. In the chapter on the bipolarity of all beings, we have seen how the two opposite poles, taken together, constitute a whole.

Even the feminine (negative) pole and the masculine (positive) pole jointly form a whole. Thus, without women, there is nothing! And without men, there is nothing! One pole by itself has no effect – like an electrical field, only the two poles working together produce energy. Something is generated, something occurs that could not have been achieved alone – something that is greater than the mere sum of both poles.

Each partner experiences for him- or herself the initial joy of the five resources and subpersonalities as well a second joy at the other's expression of those resources and even a third joy at what is produced through this exchange with the partner – a common intimacy, a spirit of eroticism, passionate nights, a feeling of being cared for, and intellectual discoveries.

Multiplying these joys and resources together, we arrive at 3 x 5 = 15 joys. These are the 15 joys that contribute to health and cement each partner relationship.

Whoever can make all inner wealth come alive of its own accord will find abundance wherever he is and paradise wherever he goes.
ANONYMOUS

Personal paradise and paradise as a couple are possible

Humans have always harbored the desire to return to paradise. Of course, we can never go back to the beginning, whether to an untouched natural paradise or to the warmth and total caring of the womb.

Yet, while we cannot go back, there is in fact a paradise if we go forward! And achieving it lies within our own power! It is a matter of becoming aware of what our own paradise (as distinct from other people's) looks like and how it can be realized.

All men and women are entitled by their true nature to live a heavenly life, provided they are ready to invest their resources in it. In addition to the 15 joys already discussed, there are a few more joys that are germane to achieving a beautiful and enjoyable life:

- Joy in one's children
- Professional fulfillment (career as a calling)
- Good food
- Fitness, athletics, care of one's body
- Good living
- Living in a beautiful home
- A lovely garden
- Freedom and independence within a permanent relationship
- Friends appropriate to one's own identity
- Variety
- Renewal
- Creativity
- Relaxation and suitable forms of leisure and vacation

Since others cannot imagine or know what we need, this means that we must take our own initiative to claim those needs, develop them, and custom-tailor our own life. It is important for us to guarantee our well-being and ensure that all our true needs and desires are fulfilled.

We cannot wait for serendipitous destiny to supply us with everything. Many people believe that only that which happens coincidentally is of value; they experience less joy in having to demand or work at things. In their eyes, this does not count as 'happiness'. For this reason, most people are still "waiting for Santa Claus", as Eric Berne puts it.

They do not understand that it is precisely through waiting or spending time on the periphery of their being that they attract misfortune – the exact opposite of what they expected. As the saying goes, "Nothing comes from nothing." Yet it is even worse: what comes from nothing is usually unhappiness and misfortune! Destiny provides the energy that was repressed. Every failure to deploy one's talents and energy comes back like a boomerang! Waiting, therefore, is linked to several different negative outcomes:

- Not doing a job
- Having no friends, feeling lonely
- Living where one does not truly feel at home
- Having many partner-related problems and conflicts
- Contracting an illness that reduces the enjoyment of life

What can be done, then, to shift out of a waiting posture and achieve personal paradise? It is important to seize the initiative and adapt everything to ourselves. We must assemble the mosaic of our own life from a multiplicity of individual tiles to achieve the destiny we desire. How we do this is illustrated by the simple examples that follow:

If I want to win at sports, I need to train.

I make sure I always eat food that is tasty and healthy.

I assert free range of action.

I only bring technical devices into my life that make me happy.

I manage and organize my own life.

I make sure that my sexual needs are satisfied.

I practice material, physical, emotional, and intellectual cleanliness.

I show my feelings.

I make sure that my erotic needs are satisfied.

I create beauty in my surroundings, my attire, my home, my garden, etc.

I have transformed my old outdated beliefs into beliefs that match reality.

I have my own life program and my own path. I read books and further my education.

I am educated and have many intellectual friends.

I travel to countries that have cultures and lifestyles that interest me.

I make sure I achieve my own goals.

My life is no longer directed by conventional morality and convention but by ethical principles of living.

I am accepting of my ideas and I incorporate change and variety into my life.

I enjoy my leisure time and have good friends.

I conquer my cravings and find alternatives to them. I achieve all my desires and dreams.

From these and other joys, we select the ones that suit us and place them into our 'shopping cart.' Blessed with this abundance, we can then live a literally joyful life. As Voltaire has written, "Paradise is where I am."

Two people, each of whom has mastered the art of creating paradise for themselves, can say to each other, "Come on, let's make it beautiful!"

The result they can achieve in this process is something that is just a dream for so many others: a paradise for two!

Appendix

Explanation of terms

Superego:

The standard of good and evil is synonymous with the learned conscience and the superego. The superego is a psychic agency formed by childhood impressions, parental influences, and other societal forces. It develops through the introjection of societal norms, requirements, commands, and prohibitions into the psychological world. It does not matter here whether the respective norms or taboos are expressly stated. This inner control system implanted in the individual by one's parents and other adult authority figures demands obedience.

Collective neurosis (second nature):

The nature imposed on a person. The essence of collective neurosis is that human resources and capacities are inhibited in their development by norms. This blockage results in what are known as defense and adaptive mechanisms that collectively form the second nature. In the world of collective neurosis, the person no longer strives to develop his or her resources and capacities but only seeks substitutes (surrogate culture).

True nature (first nature):

An individual's true nature, hidden under the artificial superstructure of the second nature. By developing the talents and capacities bestowed by nature, the individual allows his or her energies to flow freely, in this way engaging in active prevention of misfortune.

Overview: reactive feelings (substitute feelings)

The following table lists substitutions for our reactive feelings. Such feelings are understood to mean replacement feelings. This means that they take the place of true feelings, needs, and energies that are not or cannot be activated for a variety of reasons.

Feeling(s) …	*substitute for …*
anger, aggression	initiative, audacity, activity, sports, implementation, assertiveness, self-assuredness
envy	developing business skills, attending success, seminars, getting more enjoyment out of life, consistently pursuing one's own goals

feelings of confinement	claiming one's own (free) range of action, developing rhetorical skills to express oneself more freely and be better able to handle difficult situations
depression	developing psychological character, summoning greater courage to express one's identity, being free from the control of others, questioning of old norms and ideals as well as morality and convention
hate	experiencing love, sexuality, and passion, developing entrepreneurial skills, starting one's own business or company, being independent, learning management skills, developing one's own creativity
frustration	analyzing oneself and one's circumstances to recognize what to change in one's own life
feeling of dissonance	harmonizing content and form, compensating oneself – i.e., bringing oneself into harmony, expressing one's own tastes, making things beautiful and pleasing for oneself
feelings of powerlessness	development of self-concept, achieving one's ideas and plans, going one's own way
futility	further education, reading books, attending lectures and seminars, finding one's own meaning of life
guilt feelings	resolving earlier norms and ideals, designing one's own code of conduct, becoming aware of one's own right to exist and human rights, skills development, being one's own judge
nervousness	developing the skill to become independent and free, discovering how to gradually lift many burdens and achieve greater leisure time and relaxation
feelings of anxiety	developing the skill to detect backgrounds, gathering more information, constructively developing one`s own fantasy, discerning and realizing alternative approaches beyond convention and morality

Table of needs:

The 144 human needs

It is important to ask ourselves which of these real needs has already been satisfied, and which have not.

This catalog of needs, which makes no claim to completeness, provides a good tool for you to discover where you stand. You can use it to stimulate self-reflection.

	satisfied	partially satisfied	not satisfied
Need for assertiveness and self-affirmation	☐	☐	☐
Need to be egoistic	☐	☐	☐
Need to display valor and moral courage	☐	☐	☐
Need to compete and win	☐	☐	☐
Need to lead (take over leadership)	☐	☐	☐
Need to be involved in athletics	☐	☐	☐
Need to acquire	☐	☐	☐
Need to get started with something	☐	☐	☐
Need to do one`s own thing	☐	☐	☐
Need to accomplish pioneering work	☐	☐	☐
Need to create a pilot project	☐	☐	☐
Need to take action	☐	☐	☐

Need for one`s own turf	☐	☐	☐
Need for one`s own room	☐	☐	☐
Need for boundaries	☐	☐	☐
Need to find and keep one`s place	☐	☐	☐
Need to have value	☐	☐	☐
Need for self-worth	☐	☐	☐

Need to enjoy life	☐	☐	☐
Need for good-tasting, high-quality food	☐	☐	☐
Need for one`s own lifestyle	☐	☐	☐
Need to stockpile supplies	☐	☐	☐
Need to protect oneself (need for security)	☐	☐	☐
Need to be poltically active	☐	☐	☐
Need to showcase oneself	☐	☐	☐
Need for movement	☐	☐	☐
Need to take short trips	☐	☐	☐
Need to speak	☐	☐	☐
Need to write	☐	☐	☐
Need to absorb and share information	☐	☐	☐
Need for one`s own free range of action	☐	☐	☐
Need to surf the internet	☐	☐	☐
Need to be up to date with technology	☐	☐	☐

Need to be reachable anywhere by mobile phone	☐	☐	☐
Need to learn something new	☐	☐	☐
Need to work with one`s hands and make crafts	☐	☐	☐
Need to be accepted	☐	☐	☐
Need for physical closeness and cuddling	☐	☐	☐
Need to have one`s own home	☐	☐	☐
Need for homeland	☐	☐	☐
Need for personal privacy	☐	☐	☐
Need for psychological warmth	☐	☐	☐
Need for tenderness	☐	☐	☐
Need for security	☐	☐	☐
Need to give and receive caring	☐	☐	☐
Need to have a family	☐	☐	☐
Need for oral sex	☐	☐	☐
Need to experience nature	☐	☐	☐

Need for sexuality	☐	☐	☐
Need for one `s own children	☐	☐	☐
Need for autonomy	☐	☐	☐
Need for start one `s own business or company	☐	☐	☐
Need to undertake something	☐	☐	☐
Need to play	☐	☐	☐
Need to manage one `s own life	☐	☐	☐
Need to act	☐	☐	☐
Need to be in the spotlight	☐	☐	☐

Need for pleasure and fun	☐	☐	☐
Need to organize	☐	☐	☐
Need to delegate	☐	☐	☐
Need to clean	☐	☐	☐
Need for cleanliness in one `s surroundings	☐	☐	☐
Need to show one `s own feelings	☐	☐	☐
Need to criticize	☐	☐	☐
Need to analyze	☐	☐	☐
Need to make distinctions, differentiate, and go into detail	☐	☐	☐
Need to conserve energies and resources	☐	☐	☐
Need to adapt	☐	☐	☐
Need for a job that suit `s one own nature	☐	☐	☐
Need to adjust to environmental conditions	☐	☐	☐
Need to deal with health and illness	☐	☐	☐
Need for reutilization (recycling)	☐	☐	☐
Need for harmony and peace	☐	☐	☐
Need for beauty and taste	☐	☐	☐
Need for eroticism	☐	☐	☐
Need to be desired	☐	☐	☐
Need to make the most out of one `s attractiveness	☐	☐	☐

Need to campaign for one`s cause	☐	☐	☐
Need to gain advantage	☐	☐	☐
Need to express one`s own tastes	☐	☐	☐
Need for encounters and partner relationships	☐	☐	☐
Need to be able to choose people and goods from a variety of possible options	☐	☐	☐
Need to reconcile content and form	☐	☐	☐
Need to be strategic and tactical (diplomatic)	☐	☐	☐
Need to gather knowledge	☐	☐	☐
Need for power	☐	☐	☐
Need for self-determination	☐	☐	☐
Need to go one`s own way	☐	☐	☐
Need to commit oneself, to form a solid partner relationship	☐	☐	☐
Need to achieve one`s sexual fantasies	☐	☐	☐
Need to create concepts	☐	☐	☐
Need to form a personal opinion	☐	☐	☐
Need to plan	☐	☐	☐
Need to develop one`s own ideas	☐	☐	☐
Need for one`s own intellectual property	☐	☐	☐
Need for transformation	☐	☐	☐
Need to evangelize	☐	☐	☐

Need to travel	☐	☐	☐
Need to explore other cultures	☐	☐	☐
Need for one`s own world view	☐	☐	☐
Need for one`s own philosophy of life	☐	☐	☐
Need to expand	☐	☐	☐
Need to improve one`s own partner relationship	☐	☐	☐
Need to spend time abroad	☐	☐	☐
Need to nurture and be nurtured (to experience joy)	☐	☐	☐

Need to continue one`s education	☐	☐	☐
Need to make one`s own sense of things	☐	☐	☐
Need to experience refined things (opera, concerts, exhibit openings)	☐	☐	☐
Need for career success (to rise in the organization)	☐	☐	☐
Need to be recognized for something important and significant	☐	☐	☐
Need to be able to concentrate on something	☐	☐	☐
Need to accomplish one`s goals and take responsibility	☐	☐	☐
Need to be able to plan one`s time (schedule oneself)	☐	☐	☐
Need for punctuality	☐	☐	☐
Need for dependability	☐	☐	☐
Need to discover and experience one`s own vocation	☐	☐	☐
Need to live in accordance with the ethics of life	☐	☐	☐
Need to discover and live out one`s own rights	☐	☐	☐
Need to assume responsibility	☐	☐	☐
Need to be given the right	☐	☐	☐
Need for order, rules, and control	☐	☐	☐
Need for freedom	☐	☐	☐
Need for distance	☐	☐	☐
Need for independence	☐	☐	☐
Need for variety	☐	☐	☐
Need to experience something new	☐	☐	☐
Need to take advantage of special offers (hunt bargains)	☐	☐	☐
Need for adventure	☐	☐	☐
Need for leisure time	☐	☐	☐
Need to establish and maintain friendships	☐	☐	☐
Need to rise above the crowd, be someone special	☐	☐	☐
Need to reform and renew something	☐	☐	☐
Need to make an exception for oneself	☐	☐	☐

Need for peace and quiet	☐	☐	☐
Need to become involved in social issues, to assist others	☐	☐	☐
Need to investigate backgrounds	☐	☐	☐
Need to explore the unconscious	☐	☐	☐
Need to find alternatives	☐	☐	☐
Need for secrecy	☐	☐	☐
Need to expose pretense and lies	☐	☐	☐
Need for spiritual experiences	☐	☐	☐
Need to learn about the beyond	☐	☐	☐
Need to comprehend the world beyond good and evil	☐	☐	☐
Need to expand one`s awareness	☐	☐	☐
Need to give expression to one`s own fantasy	☐	☐	☐

The ten laws of destiny

1. The law of development

The sage Ostanes has masterfully described the developmental phases of humans and humanity:

One nature delights in another nature

One nature conquers another nature

One nature dominates another nature

Similarly, one can observe different phases of development in each human life. This becomes clear from the example of a book that we re-read after having initially read it perhaps ten or twenty years before, this time discovering that we assess it differently now than we did back then. If, upon first reading, we wrote notes in the margin or highlighted certain passages, these now offer us an opportunity to see how our own awareness has developed because of our accumulated experience. What once seemed important to us may now seem insignificant, while we now consider other sections as especially meaningful. This difference in perception and discernment reflects our own development of awareness. This model of awareness development can be generally extrapolated from the reading of a book to all knowledge and every judgment, whether concerning ideas on happiness, love, God, or the quality of life.

2. The law of cause and effect

Instead of taking responsibility for their own thoughts, feelings, and actions, many people attribute these resources to certain ideas about coincidence, luck, or even karmic entanglements. In doing so, they do not acknowledge that the law of action and reaction applies everywhere and at all times. This means that such details as body posture, dress, manner of speaking, status symbols, or feelings trigger specific reactions in their own surroundings. The reactions of others to something we say or do usually appear unconnected to our own actions – or, put another way, they seem to be actions that affect us without having been caused by any action on our part; all too often, these are experienced and perceived as unfair hardship. Those who fail to understand how their environment reacts to them and affects them are like a leaf in the wind; their destiny is clouded.

3. The law of balance

Balance is frequently illustrated by a mechanical scale with two counterbalanced pans. As one pan falls, the other rises, creating an imbalance. This occurs when one of the weighing pans overcompensates the other because the latter can no longer match what the former requires. In this example, harmony and balance are equalized in up and down as well as in the resting position of the two weighing pans. This symbolizes absolute balance in motion as well as at rest. The symbol of the scale is very instructive in explaining the logic of polarity. This is because polarity expresses how the two poles form one pair. The upward and downward motion of the weighing pans are a single movement, since one results from the other and vice versa. Up is not possible without down. This is equally valid for any imaginable polarity.

4. The law of the return of the repressed

Closely connected with the law of balance is the law of the return of the repressed. Through repression, contents are not simply deleted from our inner life; rather, they remain dormant there and return at another time. They are unconsciously projected onto other people and material objects that symbolize the repressed potential. It is relevant here that, in contrast to Freudian psychoanalysis, it is not only sexual energies that are repressed into the unconscious: all human resources, energies, and capacities that should be at one's disposal can fall victim to the process of repression.

Moreover, it is important to see that all energy becomes perverted by the act of repression. Hence, energy appears not in its usual garb but generally in a distorted, frequently unrecognizable form. Because of this, it is not easy for us to discern that our own repressed issues are now primary, that the cause of so much pain is nothing other than an unrealized subpersonality or an undeveloped resource or capability that we are now destined to endure passively.

For example, if a man represses his assertive energy, this act gives rise to aggression. This perverted assertive energy is now unconsciously projected, and he is left to deal constantly with an aggressive partner. In this manner, he experiences his own assertive energy as suffering. A man who is assertive and could therefore more easily get along with such a woman will never have to confront such a situation in the first place.

5. The law of affinity

The law of affinity states that a relationship or correspondence exists between the inner world and the outer world, that what we encounter on the outside also lives within us, that the external symbols surrounding us are reflections of our inner lives. Or, to put it another way, everything we harbor within ourselves, everything that our spirit contains, is essentially projected onto a screen, where it appears in the form of other people, symbols, and occurrences. We are everywhere surrounded with ourselves. An individual can recognize his or her unconscious and conscious projections in this process. The external projections make clear what the individual looks like. Thus, it is not crucial what someone says but rather how this appears in his or her world.

6. The law of attraction

The unconscious is not only responsible for illness and health – it also affects the external world. On the outside, it attracts what corresponds to the inner world, resulting in an affinity (law of affinity) and attracting to its own deficiency the corresponding opposite pole (law of balance) or allowing repressed issues to return (law of the return of the repressed).

What are the other factors that influence this attraction mechanism and determine the frequency of the attraction? Besides prenatal conditioning, the environment in which one grew up, the education one received, and birth order, these primarily include one's biographical situation and the compulsive repetition whereby certain behavior patterns are exhibited over and over in the same fashion.

7. The law of affirmation

All of us would like to have the feeling that our life path is the correct one, that what we think and feel is proper, that how we behave and act is acceptable. In this way, everyone unconsciously searches one's environment for affirmation. The law of affirmation states that every belief, attitude, preference, opinion, judgment, feeling, criterion, norm, ideal, and scientific hypothesis or theory is always self-affirmed.

8. The law of positive and negative reinforcement

The law of positive and negative reinforcement is closely linked to the law of affirmation. Each affirmation of a position or behavior is simultaneously linked to a reinforcement. Destiny will positively reinforce those who have developed a resource or skill. If the resource is not developed or is present only in a perverted form, there is a tendency toward negative reinforcement.

9. The law of thought and belief

First a comment: in many cases, the law of thought and belief does not have the effect that it is assumed to have. Negative thinkers and pessimists do not always attract the negative, nor do positive thinkers and optimists consistently attract the positive. Since the reality of life is different, it is inevitable that the unconscious will also function differently. It is a question of using the conscious, not to program the unconscious – which is a contradiction in itself – but rather to reveal the unconscious program and, if necessary, to make changes in it to bring about a beneficial destiny.

10. The law of content and form

The law of content and form states that emotional and intellectual content must also assume a corresponding external form to achieve a pleasing destiny. If, for example, an individual has a progressive political stance, it would be good for him or her to express this inner progressiveness on the outside – perhaps through an appropriate style of attire, home furnishings, or landscaping. If such a person were instead to have a liking for conservative trappings, there would be a dissonance between content and form, thus inviting a negative destiny due to his or her inability to attract compatible partners or friends. People will be prone to form mistaken opinions about such a person, who will not seem authentic to them. This leads to distorted reality, misinterpretations, and responses based on false impressions.

Bibliography

Alfred Adler: The Neurotic Constitution: Outlines of a Comparative Individualistic Psychology and Psychotherapy, New York, 1917

Eric Berne: What Do You Say After You Say Hello? The Psychology of Human Destiny, New York, 1983

Doris Bischof-Köhler: Von Natur aus anders, Stuttgart, 2011

Angelika Förster: Glückstankstellen, Munich, 2013

Sigmund Freud, Totem and Taboo, New York, 1913

Nicolas Guéguen, Archives of Sexual Behavior (2015) 44: 2227. https://doi.org/10.1007/s10508-014-0422-z

Carl Jung: Collected Works, Princeton, 1981

Otto Mainzer: Die sexuelle Zwangswirtschaft, Munich,1981

Hermann Meyer: Die eigene Identität, Munich, 2000

Hermann Meyer: Die Gesetze des Schicksals, Munich, 2008

Hermann Meyer: Der Jackpot des Lebens, Munich, 2009

Hermann Meyer: Das Drehbuch des Lebens, Munich, 2010

Anne Moir, David Jessel: Brain Sex: The Real Difference Between Men and Women, New York, 1991

René A. Spitz, W. Godfrey Cobliner: First Year of Life: A Psychoanalytic Study of Normal and Deviant Development of Object Relations, New York, 1966

Claude Steiner: A Warm Fuzzy Tale, Fawnskin, 1977

Stefan Woinoff: Überlisten Sie Ihr Beuteschema, Munich, 2007

DISCLAIMER

The advice in this book has been carefully weighed and reviewed by the author and publisher. Nevertheless, it does not claim to be a substitute for competent medical advice. Each reader is responsible for his or her own treatment. Consequently, all information in this book is presented without warranty or guarantee of any kind by the author or the publisher. The author's and publisher's liability for personal injury, material damage, and financial loss is excluded.

[*] In boys, the analogous development to the Electra complex in girls is the Oedipus complex, defined as the boy's development of feelings of love and sexual desire toward his mother, particularly the urge to have her entirely for himself.

Printed in Poland
by Amazon Fulfillment
Poland Sp. z o.o., Wrocław

74546837R00090